Collecting Child Support

Collecting Child Support
12 Effective Strategies

Gregory C. Damman, J.D.

Self-Counsel Press Inc.
a subsidiary of
International Self-Counsel Press Ltd.
U.S.A.   Canada

Printed in Canada

First edition: November 1997

Cataloging in Publication Data

Damman, Gregory C., 1963-
    Collecting child support

    (Self-Counsel legal series)
    ISBN 1-55180-127-2

    1. Child support—Law and legislation—United States
    —Popular works.   I. Title. II. Series.
    KF549.Z9D36 1997   346.7301'72   C97-910672-9

Self-Counsel Press Inc.
a subsidiary of
International Self-Counsel Press Ltd.

1704 N. State Street   1481 Charlotte Road
Bellingham, WA 98225   North Vancouver, BC V7J 1H1
U.S.A.   Canada

To my wife, Susie,
and my children, Elizabeth and Ethan

Contents

1 A map   1

   a.   Think positive   4

   b.   Educate yourself   6

   c.   Be realistic   8

2 Finding the payor on the map   9

   a.   The absent parent   10

   b.   Public and private records   10

     1.   Finding a Social Security number   11

     2.   Using a Social Security number   12

     3.   Using the U.S. Postal Service   15

     4.   Accessing motor vehicle records   15

     5.   Accessing public business records   17

     6.   Obtaining voter registration records   18

     7.   Searching for hunting and fishing licenses   18

     8.   A note about public records   18

c.	The payor's family	19
d.	High-tech sleuthing	19
e.	Hiring a pro	21

3 The wage withholding order — cruising the interstate 23
a.	Payors who work for someone else	25
b.	Payors who are self-employed	27
c.	Play your best cards	28

4 License revocation — a new road 31
a.	Lost without a license	31
	1. Driver's license	33
	2. Professional license	34
	3. Recreational license	36
	4. Passports	37
	5. Other licenses	38
b.	Payor's right to appeal	38

5 The property lien — traveling a difficult road 41
a.	Creating and enforcing property liens	41
	1. Real estate	42
	2. Personal property	43
b.	Who benefits from a lien?	45
c.	Getting an advance lien	46
d.	Liens as locators	47
e.	A final note about liens	47

6 Computer as travel guide 49
| a. | A powerful collection tool | 49 |
| b. | Getting on the Internet | 50 |

c. Putting the Internet to work   53

   1. Search directories   54

   2. Locators and notifiers   55

   3. Public and private records   56

   4. Agency links   57

   5. Usenet — networking with others   59

d. Computers behind the scenes   60

7 Intercepting an income tax refund   63

a. Leave the driving to the government   63

b. Tax refund interception basics   64

c. How to participate in the tax refund
   interception program   64

d. The mechanics of tax refund interception   65

e. Interception strategy   66

f. Intercepting lottery money   68

8 Paternity and the unmarried payor   69

a. A different starting point   69

b. Presumptions and the law   70

c. Establishing paternity   71

d. Preparing for a paternity case   73

e. Settlement agreements   74

f. Benefits of establishing paternity   75

g. Visitation   76

h. New agency power   77

i. If you already have a paternity
   settlement agreement   78

9 Agency caseworkers: overworked tour guides 79

   a. Too busy to help? 79

   b. Agency history 80

   c. Agency overload 81

   d. Increased agency power 82

   e. Tips on dealing with a state agency 83

      1. Minimize agency homework 84

      2. Act immediately 85

      3. Be the squeaky wheel 85

      4. Be patient, truthful, and polite 86

   f. Private agencies 87

10 Modifying child support orders 95

   a. Stale orders 95

   b. Fraudulent orders 98

   c. Reverse modification 99

11 Hiring a lawyer 101

   a. A high-priced travel agent 101

   b. When to hire a lawyer 102

      1. Pre-order lawyer 103

      2. Post-order lawyer 104

   c. Finding a lawyer 106

   d. The squeaky wheel theory 108

12 Good things to know 109

   a. Last-minute packing 109

   b. The importance of allowing visitation 109

   c. Bankruptcy 110

   d. Crossing state lines 111

e.	Grandparent liability	112
f.	Payors not in the country	112
g.	Don't let success fool you	113

Appendixes

1	Child support collection survey checklist	115
2	Child support collection map	117
3	Child support collection survey	125
4	Federal and state child support enforcement agencies	133

Samples

#1	Letter Requesting Payor's Driving Abstract	16
#2	Letter Requesting Information From Payor's Family Member	20
#3	Case Initiation Letter	88
#4	Case Follow-up Letter	90

Notice to readers

Laws are constantly changing. Every effort is made to keep this publication as current as possible. However, the author, the publisher, and the vendor of this book make no representation or warranties regarding the outcome or the use to which the information in this book is put and are not assuming any liability for any claims, losses, or damages arising out of the use of this book. The reader should not rely on the author or the publisher of this book for any professional advice. Please be sure that you have the most recent edition.

Note: The fees quoted in this book are correct at the date of publication. However, fees are subject to change without notice. For current fees, please check with the court registry or appropriate government office nearest you.

1

A map

Suppose you had plans to take a long and arduous trip that would take you through unfamiliar territory. Would you feel comfortable leaving home without a map to follow? Probably not. Collecting child support is a little bit like taking a trip into unfamiliar territory. You need a map to follow in order to do the job right. This book was written to help you find your way through the child support collection process.

Unpaid child support is a serious problem, and the consequences of getting lost during an effort to collect it may be severe: you may not be able to provide the things for your child that are essential for his or her proper development. Supplying adequate food, proper clothing, medical care, college savings, and many other important items are often possible only if child support is paid.

Planning this trip into child support collection requires a lot of thinking, planning, and good old-fashioned hard work.

Because of the effort involved, collecting child support may seem daunting. After several unsuccessful attempts to collect past-due support, you might be tempted to give up. However, having a map to follow can keep you from going off course, losing your way, and giving up. After all, a map can easily get you back on course when you lose your way, and it will give you the confidence you need to continue your efforts.

If you need any motivation to follow a child support map, just think about how much better off your children will be if you are able to collect their child support. Your child support collection map (see Appendix 2), combined with a positive attitude and approach, will work together to provide for your children's well-being — now, and for many years into the future. Instead of tearing the worksheet found in Appendix 2 out of the book, you may want to photocopy it, so that it is easier to carry with you on your collection journey.

If your child support has gone unpaid for several months (or years), before doing anything else, you should sit down and create a map for getting the money collected. Your map should not be something that you store in your head and retrieve from time to time when you feel like making a half-hearted effort to collect the money your children so badly need.

It is very important to be organized. Create a file and place all your papers related to your child support order in it. The file — your child support collection map — should be your most important source when you are working toward getting your overdue child support collected. This map is unique in that it not only helps you get where you're going but it also summarizes where you've been. Your map should contain at least the following:

(a) Your original child support order and any subsequent order modifying it

(b) The payor's* current name, address, and telephone number

(c) The current name, address, and telephone number of the payor's employer

(d) The payor's Social Security number

(e) Your local child support collection agency's address and telephone number

(f) Your lawyer's name, address, and telephone number

(g) A chronological summary of all steps you have taken to collect your child support, including names, addresses, and telephone numbers of all persons contacted

(h) A current printout of the status of your child support account, including dates of payments, missed payments, and total amount unpaid

(i) The payor's driver's license number

(j) A list of all assets owned by the payor and the value of those assets

(k) The name, address, and telephone number of the office in charge of administering any professional license the payor may hold

(l) Any ideas you may have for future collection efforts

You may want to add more items to this list. The purpose of having all of this information in a file is so that you may quickly access it when you need to refresh your memory on steps already taken, and to be taken. Your map will also be of great help to anyone with whom you may later deal in attempting to collect child support, such as lawyers and agency caseworkers. These people will be more effective in helping you if you are able to simply copy your file for them, thereby eliminating needless duplication of your efforts. In

---

* Throughout this book, the parent with a child support obligation is referred to as the payor. You, as the collector, are the payee.

some cases, a child support map can reduce lawyer's fees by enabling your lawyer to focus only on areas that you have not yet explored.

Keep your map in a safe and handy place, such as a filing cabinet or drawer in your house, so that you will always know where to turn when a child support collection question arises.

After you have prepared your child support collection map, you should take some time to lay the groundwork for a successful collection effort; you will benefit greatly from getting yourself into the right frame of mind, educating yourself about the child support collection process, and taking a realistic look at what you want to accomplish.

a. Think positive

Many parents who are owed child support make diligent attempts to collect the money over long periods, but continually run into roadblocks that prevent them from ever seeing the fruits of their labors. It's easy to see how these parents can become frustrated and fall into a negative state of mind. It is not easy to continue to work at a project that never seems to bear any fruit, especially when there are constant reminders of pressing financial burdens.

To further compound matters, the negative feedback may be made worse by other pressures that are indirectly related to the inability to collect child support. For example, if food, clothing, medical care, and other items vital to a child's well-being are unavailable or in short supply because child support payments are not being made, a parent is forced to seek other ways to provide these necessities. Often, the only place to turn is public assistance programs, which may cause a parent to feel that he or she has failed because welfare programs are needed to support a child. Reliance on these public assistance programs can create a complacency that may stifle the energy you need for your child support collection efforts.

In order to have the energy and positive attitude needed to make a commitment to collecting unpaid child support, you must not let yourself fall into a negative state of mind which may cause you to give up hope that you will ever collect the money that is owed. As you work on collecting child support, always remember that the next phone call, the next letter, or the next computer search could trigger a flow of payments and the end of your collection worries. There are countless examples of parents who were about to give up on collecting child support but made yet another attempt and were able to uncover a collection avenue that ultimately led to payment in full.

In order to keep a positive state of mind, keep a list in your map file that details all of the things you could provide for your children if past due and current child support payments were made. Braces for their teeth? New bicycles? New winter coats? Chances are, the list will be quite long. You may also want to make a list of all the things that you could do with the extra time that you would have available if you were able to end your child support collection efforts.

Try to locate other people who are also having difficulty collecting their child support and share stories, resources, and collection suggestions with them. By networking, you gain the advantage of having another person review your situation and provide pointers on subjects that may never have crossed your mind. Sometimes, a collection tip from a friend who takes a fresh look at your case can energize you when you have fallen into a rut.

Finding someone with similar collection problems with whom you could discuss child support collection matters was difficult in the past. Today, however, the widespread use of the Internet has made it easier to find other people with whom you can share ideas. For example, you can surf the

Internet and locate other people with whom you may be able to exchange e-mail messages about specific collection problems and issues. For more detailed information on using the Internet to assist with your child support collection efforts, see chapter 6.

b. Educate yourself

No matter how much effort you put into collecting child support, you may never see a dime unless you know how to properly channel your efforts. The key to properly channeling your efforts is to educate yourself about the *entire* child support collection process. The word entire is emphasized because knowing how to collect child support involves much more than just knowing how to request a wage withholding order or file a motion to have the payor held in contempt of court. You need to understand the psychology of child support collection, including the mind-set of the payor. The more you know about the entire collection process, the better your chances of recovering unpaid child support.

Educating yourself about the entire child support collection process is akin to locating your starting point on a map. Locating your starting position on the map is the first step toward getting you to your destination.

To begin building the foundation of your knowledge about the child support collection process, you must first review the most important document in your file: your child support order. Read it, and then read it again. After you have read it twice, read it a third time. You should be able to recite its provisions without looking at it. Once you are familiar with the terms of your child support order, it's a good idea to review any additional documents related to the order, such as correspondence from lawyers, other court orders, and papers related to the payor's employment and assets.

6

Another important document to have and to carefully review is a current printout of the status of your child support payments. This printout should include a list detailing every missed payment, the payments made, and the total amount owed to date plus interest. You should be able to obtain this printout from the clerk of the court that issued your child support order. It is a good idea to periodically get an updated copy of this printout so that you always know the status of your payments.

After you are familiar with the details of your own child support situation, you should move on to educating yourself about the various ways that you can collect past-due child support. That, of course, is the primary purpose of this book.

Finally, your educational journey should lead you into a career as an amateur psychologist. That is, you need to learn what factors cause a person to fail to pay child support. When you tell your three-year-old child to do something, and she asks why, you can often get away with simply telling her, just because. The same answer is not acceptable from a parent failing to pay child support.

There is always a reason for not paying. No doubt you have heard many of them as excuses. Your job, however, is to separate the stated reasons from the real reasons. Typically, the payor claims to be unemployed, underemployed, or to have other, more pressing, bills to pay. While these are the stated reasons, the real reason is sometimes the payor feels that you are spending the money for your own enjoyment, rather than on the children. In some cases, the payor even feels that the children have no need for the money. Given the fact that most payors feel this way, it is important to delve into the question of why they have these feelings.

Consider the possibility that you are unintentionally contributing to the payor's feeling that paying child support is not a worthwhile endeavor. Do you keep the payor informed as to what necessary items are being purchased with child support money? Do you allow visitation with the children? Do you maintain a modest standard of living for yourself so as not to create the impression that you are reaping a financial windfall from child support payments or that there is no need for it because of your apparent affluence? Take a good, hard look at these issues and try to correct any misunderstandings of the situation which may have occurred. There are subtle strategies suggested throughout this book that can help put the payor into the proper frame of mind to pay child support.

c. Be realistic

The last thing to consider as you create your child support collection map is whether you are taking a realistic approach. After all, a map with minute details on how to get to Fort Knox is of little use, because even if you get there, you cannot get your hands on any of the gold stored inside.

In other words, if the job requires a lawyer, hire a lawyer. If the job holds out absolutely no hope of success, don't waste your time with collection efforts. For example, if the payor has been severely injured in an accident and is barely surviving with government disability payments, what good does it do to pursue aggressive collection procedures if he or she can barely survive on a monthly disability check?

This, of course, is an extreme example, but there are certainly examples of other cases that involve payors who will not pay any child support. Often, this is the type of person who would rather spend time in prison for criminal nonsupport than make the required payments. If your payor falls into this category, don't waste your time. Get on with your life and find other ways to occupy your time.

2

Finding the payor on the map

According to federal statistics, approximately 85% of custodial parents are women and 15% are men. Obviously, this means that more men pay child support than women. Naturally, then, there are more men who have failed to pay child support than women. This has led to the label "deadbeat dad" to describe someone who has failed to pay child support. Care should be taken not to label all people who fail to pay child support as deadbeats. There can be legitimate reasons for not making child support payments, such as health problems, loss of a job or business, and large unexpected expenses.

It is also wrong to assume that all people who fail to pay child support are men. There are a large number of women who also have failed to pay child support, and the number is growing as gender equity takes hold in the courts and leads to more fathers with custody of their children.

a. The absent parent

Unfortunately, many people begin the child support collection process in the unenviable position of not knowing the whereabouts of the payor. This is like not knowing how to find your destination point on a map. Until you find the payor, you will never reach your goal, which is receiving payment of child support. One of life's great mysteries is how a person with the important responsibility of participating in the upbringing of his or her child can suddenly drop off the face of the earth after a child support order is entered. This is an all-too-common occurrence and is often the most frustrating part of trying to collect child support. As you deal with people who are experienced in the child support collection process, you will sometimes hear them refer to parents who cannot be found as absent parents.

Fortunately, it is becoming more and more difficult for a payor to disappear and become an absent parent. Technological tools and stronger laws designed to aid in locating absent parents combine to make it easier to locate a person who fails to pay child support. To maximize your chances of finding an absent parent, you may need to also take advantage of some traditional methods of location that have been used by private investigators for years. If you make good use of both the new and old tools, you will greatly increase your chances of locating an absent parent. Generally, parent-locating tools fall into four categories: public and private records, family resources, computer resources, and private investigators.

b. Public and private records

You have an ally in your search for the payor. Big Brother (the government) is always watching. How does Big Brother keep track of you and everyone else in the United States? With a Social Security number. Not only does the government require Social Security numbers on most types of official paperwork, but private companies also make use of them. If you know the payor's Social Security number, you may be able to request government and private company records that contain the payor's current address.

1. Finding a Social Security number

What if you don't know the payor's Social Security number? Don't worry. Chances are you have paperwork that contains the number, or if you don't, you can easily find it. Most courts now require filing paperwork which lists the payor's Social Security number in the proceeding that results in entry of a child support order. Therefore, your search for the payor's Social Security number will probably end after you locate and review the court documents in your possession. If your paperwork does not contain the payor's Social Security number, make a trip to the courthouse and ask to review the court file for your case. It is very likely that you will find some document in the court file that contains the payor's Social Security number.

If you still cannot find the payor's Social Security number after reviewing the court file, you will need to dig a little deeper. Stop and think about any business or personal transactions you took part in with the payor. For example, if you both applied for a credit card or loan, you may have had to provide your Social Security numbers on the application papers. Simply contact the lender or credit card company and request a copy of your application papers. The same may hold true for insurance policy applications and related paperwork. You could also check your children's medical records. Often, a parent's Social Security number is listed on the billing statements or medical records.

One of the most obvious sources for a Social Security number is a tax return. If you have kept copies of any of the payor's joint or separate tax returns, whether state or federal, these documents will definitely contain the payor's Social Security number. If you don't have copies of tax returns and you previously filed a joint return with the payor, you may want to request a copy of the filed return from the IRS. To get a copy of your previously filed tax return, you can go to your local IRS office and request Form 4506 along with its instructions. Fill out the form, send it in, and you should have a copy of your return within a few weeks. There is a $23[*] fee for returns from each tax year that you request.

The Personal Responsibility and Work Opportunity Reconciliation Act of 1996 (referred to in this book as the 1996 Welfare Reform Act) is a mandate for broad and sweeping changes in the way in which child support is collected in the United States. One of the changes made by this act is that all applications for professional licenses, commercial driver's licenses, occupational licenses, and marriage licenses are required to list the applicant's Social Security number. Therefore, these public licenses will be a good source for finding the payor's Social Security number.

2. Using a Social Security number

After you have found the payor's Social Security number, the next step is to put that number to work for you. A good way to use a Social Security number to locate a payor is to go directly to your local child support enforcement agency office (CSE), provide a caseworker with the number, and ask to have the payor located. The CSE caseworker should have plenty of location tools available, including a State Parent Locator Service (SPLS) which enables him or her to search the records of other states. You may also request a Federal Parent Locator Service (FPLS) search, which is a search of the current address records of the IRS, Department of Defense, National Personnel Records Center, Social Security Administration,

---

[*] Note that all fees are subject to change without notice. Please check all fees with your local IRS office before submitting funds.

Department of Veterans Affairs, and State Employment Security Agencies.

If your local child support enforcement agency is either too busy or unable to find the payor by using a Social Security number, consider farming out this chore to an expert. There are numerous companies that offer specialized investigative services to the public, including assistance in locating people. One of the services these companies provide involves a Social Security number search which often returns a current address for the number holder. A request for a search of this type is typically processed in a matter of days. Given that you could spend a lot of time and energy on location efforts, it is usually a good idea to take advantage of professional assistance if you can afford it. The fee for this service usually runs between $15 and $60, with no apparent reason for the price difference. You may want to call one of the following companies and request information on the cost and types of Social Security number address searches they provide:

International Research Bureau
1331 East Lafayette Street
Tallahassee, FL 32301
Toll-free: 1-800-447-2112

Infotel
5090 Richmond, Suite 94
Houston, TX 77056
Toll-free: 1-888-244-7761

Informus
2001 Airport Road, Suite 201
Jackson, MS 39208
Toll-free: 1-800-364-1900

There are other ways to use a Social Security number if you don't want to spend the money to hire a company to conduct a search.

If you send the Social Security Administration (SSA) a letter explaining that you have lost touch with, for example, John Smith, who used to live at 555 Jones Street, Somewhere, U.S.A., it will forward your letter to the most recent address in its files associated with that person. If your letter ends up in the hands of the payor, it's a safe bet that the payor won't immediately call you and advise you of his or her new address. However, the letter could end up in the hands of a friend or relative of the payor who is sympathetic to your plight and is willing to provide you with a current address of the payor. You should be aware, though, that the person who receives the letter could warn the payor that you are looking for him or her. The payor might then change jobs, move to a different address, or take steps to conceal his or her whereabouts. If you do decide to attempt to have a letter forwarded through the SSA, send it to the following address:

Social Security Administration
Department of Health and Human Services
6401 Security Boulevard
Baltimore, MD 21235

Another way to use the Social Security Administration to locate a payor is to conduct a search in the SSA's master death records. Since the SSA keeps track of information about all people who have died, you could arrange for a search through an investigation company to find out whether any of the payor's family member's have recently died. If so, you can then obtain a copy of the relative's obituary, which often lists the city of residence of close relatives of the deceased. This will at least provide you with a city within which to focus your search.

The companies listed earlier in this section can provide master death record searches in case you don't have a Social Security number, or if a Social Security number search on the payor is unsuccessful. You may even be able to conduct the master death record search yourself with your home computer. See chapter 6 for additional information on using your computer to locate the payor.

3. Using the U.S. Postal Service

Lawyers who collect money for their clients have long known a simple trick that often enables them to locate people who seem to have disappeared. It's called a postal search. The U.S. Postal Service keeps track of forwarding addresses so that it can forward mail to its customers. The forwarding address information is available to anyone who requests it. You simply go to the post office, fill out a form listing the payor's last address, and for a small fee, request the payor's forwarding address. A postal search, of course, will work only if the payor recently moved and left a forwarding address.

Another way to take advantage of U.S. Postal Service forwarding orders is to simply mail an envelope to the payor's last known address and write "Do not forward, address correction requested" on it. If the payor has moved and left a forwarding address, you will receive the envelope back with the payor's forwarding address on it.

4. Accessing motor vehicle records

Many states allow public access to the driving records of its citizens. If you know which state the payor lives in, you can request a copy of his or her driving abstract from the state department of motor vehicles. This report may show that the payor was recently in an automobile accident or cited for a traffic offense. If so, you can arrange to get a copy of either the accident report or the citation, both of which should contain the payor's current address. There may be a small fee for this service.

Sample #1 is a letter that you could use to make such a request. Before sending the letter, you should call the Department of Motor Vehicles and talk to someone in the driver's records department. Verify the address to which the request should be sent and the amount of money to enclose with

September 8, 199-

Mary Parent
758 Bond Street
Anytown, MI 48900
(517) 769-0000

Driver's Records Department
State of Michigan, Department of Motor Vehicles
200 Lincoln Drive
Anytown, MI 48901

Dear Records Clerk:

I am in need of the driving abstract for John Parent. Please send the abstract to me at the above address. I am enclosing $15 as payment of the fee for this service. You may call me at 769-0000 if you have any questions about this request. Thank you.

Sincerely,

Mary Parent

Mary Parent

your request, and find out what information to include in your request. Most states will want the person's name, date of birth, and Social Security number. Keep in mind that even though the report may contain an address for the payor, that address might not be current if the payor has moved since last renewing his or her driver's license.

5. Accessing public business records

The payor may also be located through public business records. This is often a good source if the payor is self-employed. A self-employed parent is not tied to a particular job and may be inclined to pull up roots and secretly move to another location, hoping to get a fresh start in business away from your watchful eye. But disappearing will be difficult if the payor is employed in a trade that requires a license. Barbers, insurance agents, realtors, lawyers, doctors, nurses, pharmacists, and many other occupations require a license. You may be able to obtain a current address for the payor by contacting the licensing department for the payor's occupation in the state in which you suspect he or she lives.

Another business-related source for locating a payor involves records that the government requires from a person conducting business. An important part of doing business relates to trademarks, trade names, patents, copyrights, corporate records, partnership records, and limited liability company records. If you know the name under which the payor does business, or a product that the payor sells, you could search the records of the Secretary of State, in the state in which the payor does business, to determine if there are registration records for a trademark or trade name. A trademark or trade name registration will contain the address of the person filing the application. If the payor recently formed a corporation, you may access corporate records through the Secretary of State's office in the state in which the corporation was formed to obtain a current address. The same holds true for certain types of partnerships and limited liability companies.

6. Obtaining voter registration records

If you know which county the payor lives in but are having trouble finding a specific address, you may contact the county election office in the county where the payor lives and obtain voter registration records. This, of course, will work only if the payor is a registered voter. If so, simply provide the election office personnel with the payor's name and date of birth, and they should be able to give you the address the payor provided when he or she registered to vote.

7. Searching for hunting and fishing licenses

Hunting and fishing are sports that are legal only with a license. Hunting and fishing license applications, like most license applications, contain the applicant's address. This type of license information is a matter of public record, and you may contact the state's fish and game commission and request a search to determine whether the payor is licensed. If so, you should be able to access the license information and obtain an address.

8. A note about public records

As you search public records, keep in mind that some records are more public than others. Don't be shy about asking a government worker, who may seem reluctant to help you, for the information contained in the records. If you don't ask, you will never receive what you want. If you do ask, the worst that can happen is that you will be refused. Even if you are refused, politely ask for an explanation for the refusal. After all, it may be that your request has been misunderstood, and after you receive the official explanation, the mistake will be discovered. Finally, even if the information is technically not allowed to be released, some government employees either ignore, or are unaware of, what type of information may be released and will tell you the payor's current address and telephone number.

c. The payor's family

As you search for the payor parent, keep in mind the adage that "you can choose your friends, but you can't choose your family." As you ponder this bit of wisdom, try to think of people who would apply it to the person from whom you are trying to collect child support. In other words, the payor may have relatives who are not especially fond of him or her and who would gladly help you if they knew your children were not receiving the support they needed. You may think that relatives who are on bad terms with the payor would not know details such as a current address, place of employment, or ownership of assets. Keep in mind, though, that information often travels indirectly through families.

The payor may think Uncle Bert is a jerk and refuse to ever talk to him, but at the same time the payor may think that Uncle Jerry is the greatest guy in the world and confide with him on every move. What if Uncle Bert is your ally but Uncle Jerry refuses to speak to you? All is not lost because Uncle Bert and Uncle Jerry may share family news about the payor, which could be available to you if you seek help from your ally, Uncle Bert. Sample #2 is a letter that could be sent to a family member of the payor to request information.

d. High-tech sleuthing

Increasing use of the Internet has opened large databases of information to many people. If you are one of the millions of people who are on-line, you may be able to locate the payor without ever leaving your home or talking to another person. Chapter 6 will address the details of using a computer to assist in your child support collection efforts. If you have

September 9, 199-

Mary Parent
758 Bond Street
Anytown, MI 48900
(517) 769-000

Bert Former In-Law
555 1st Avenue
Anytown, MI 48234

Dear Uncle Bert:

How are you and Mrs. Former In-Law? I have been busy with my job and caring for Billy, Bobby, and Betty. They are all involved in school activities and are growing up quickly. They outgrow their clothes almost as fast as I can buy them. They seem to all have Uncle Jerry's appetite! We sure miss visiting with you the way we used to when John was still around. By the way, have you heard from John? I recently tried to locate him so that I could forward some important papers to him, and could not find a current address or place of employment for him. If you know this information or can point me in the right direction, I would sure like to hear from you.

We will be in your part of the country sometime next month. If you don't mind, we will stop for a quick visit so you can see the kids. My new address and phone number are at the top of this letter in case you want to contact me. See you soon.

Best regards,

Mary

little or no experience with computer-based research and would like to take a crack at it, you should refer to chapter 6 for a primer on this subject. Even if you consider yourself a computer expert, you might want to review chapter 6 in case it contains information that you did not know about.

In a nutshell, a computer is useful in locating a payor because it provides two search methods. One method involves searching databases that could contain the payor's records, thereby giving you access to current location, employment, and asset information. The second method involves networking with other people who may be able to provide you with information about the payor.

Perhaps you do not own a computer or are intimidated by them. Do not let this stop you from gaining access to the valuable information available on the Internet. Most public libraries across the country now have computers that are available for public use and include Internet access. All you have to do is find a librarian, tell him or her what you are looking for, and ask for some assistance using the computer. If you have a computer at home, but only your children use it, ask them for help. Most children today have superb computer skills because of extensive computer use in schools. If your children can't help and you can't get to the library, ask your friends and neighbors about their computer expertise. In this day and age, it is rare not to know someone who has at least a passable amount of computer expertise. More often than not, the person you ask for help will also enjoy helping you and having the opportunity to put his or her computer knowledge to good use.

e. Hiring a pro

There are generally two types of people who hire a private investigator (PI) to find absent payors. The first type is those who have tried all of the above search techniques and still cannot find the payor. The second type is those who have the financial resources to immediately hire a PI and do so because they just don't want the hassle of trying to find the payor. Regardless of your situation, there are several things you should keep in mind before you hire a PI.

In many states, PIs are required to have licenses. You may call the state agency responsible for licensing PIs and request a list of licensed PIs in your area. Of course, the mere fact that a PI has a license does not necessarily mean that he or she is worth hiring. You should do some checking around to find out which PIs have a proven track record of results at an affordable cost. Local law enforcement officers may be able to suggest a reputable PI. In fact, when reviewing the credentials of PIs, keep in mind that those with law enforcement experience are probably more qualified than those without it. Always request detailed information about the PI's experience and background. In addition, ask for references so that you may call other people and find out whether they were satisfied with the PI's work.

After you have hired a PI, don't just sit back and wait for the results to come in. Provide the PI with as much information as possible about the payor and follow up with additional information that you might obtain later. Check in with the PI periodically and ask for updates on your case. This will help ensure that your case gets regular attention. Finally, if the PI works on the case for a few months and makes no progress, consider taking him or her off the case and sending it to a different PI. A fresh approach could help.

After you have located the payor, you are ready to begin searching for a source of money. You will have several options, including wage withholding, property liens, bank account garnishments, and income tax refund interception. Wage withholding is used frequently and is described in the next chapter.

3

The wage withholding order — cruising the interstate

When you read a road map, you probably consider a route on the interstate highways to be fast and efficient. A wage withholding order is a lot like cruising down an interstate highway. It is fast and efficient, and once you get going, there's not much that can slow you down.

It is relatively easy to put a wage withholding order to work for you. After you have located the payor, you can begin planning the best method to collect past due child support. Your first step should be to determine where the payor is employed. Later sections in this chapter describe several ways to locate a payor's place of employment. Fortunately, once you locate the payor and his or her place of employment, you are well on your way to getting a wage withholding order started. You need only make arrangements for automatic wage withholding from the payor's paycheck.

Wage withholding is perhaps the easiest way to begin getting regular payments. This collection device has been universally available since 1984, when congress passed a law mandating all states to put automatic wage withholding for child support into effect by October 1, 1985. For child support orders entered before November 1, 1990, automatic wage withholding is available when the payor owes an amount equal to 30 days of child support payments. For child support orders entered after that date through state agency action, *immediate* wage withholding is available. Immediate wage withholding is available for *all* child support orders entered after December 31, 1993, unless the parents agree to a different arrangement. You may take advantage of wage withholding yourself, through a child support collection agency, or with the assistance of your lawyer.

The amount of wages that may be withheld varies, depending on whether the payor has a second family to support. If so, the maximum amount that may be withheld is 60% of disposable earnings. If the payor does not have a second family to support, the maximum amount that may be withheld is 50% of disposable earnings. Disposable earnings are calculated in various ways by each state, but they typically are defined as gross wages, less deductions for taxes and other valid employment-related deductions.

If another creditor has a judgment against the payor and attempts to garnish the payor's wages, that creditor will have to wait until your child support payments are satisfied before being entitled to any money through garnishment. In other words, your child support order has priority because federal law has mandated collection of child support payments to be more important than collection of other debts. You should also keep in mind that your state may be one which has broadened wage withholding to include not only wages but things such as employment bonuses, unemployment compensation, workers' compensation, disability benefits, and retirement benefits.

If the payor made sporadic payments and appears to have missed payments primarily through aloofness, rather than a refusal to pay, you should suggest that the payor ask his or her employer for voluntary wage withholding. That way, your child support payments are deducted from the payor's paycheck in the same way as any other payroll deduction. If voluntary wage withholding is in place, you don't need to worry about sporadic use of wage withholding and the accompanying hassle related to requesting withholding every time the payor falls behind. Of course, since this is a voluntary arrangement, you should not make this request as a do-this-or-else demand.

Approach the subject with tact and strategy. When the payor falls behind, acknowledge that you realize he or she intended to make the payment on time, and that you understand that the payor is having difficulty finding time to sit down and write the check. After telling the payor how much your children appreciate all the past contributions, you could then suggest a voluntary wage withholding to eliminate the hassle of check writing and mailing every month. The accounting burden is placed in the payor's employer's hands.

Of course, this discussion about wage withholding will mean nothing to you unless you are first able to find out where the payor works. The manner in which you conduct your search for the payor's source of income will depend on whether the payor works for someone else or is self-employed.

a. Payors who work for someone else

In 1996, congress passed the Personal Responsibility and Work Opportunity Reconciliation Act (also known as the 1996 Welfare Reform Act). This is the new child support law that you may have heard about. The act contains provisions that make locating the place of employment of a payor who works for someone else very easy. It imposes a mandate on states to create a "new hire directory" by October 1, 1997. All employers will be required to furnish the directory with a report containing the name, address, and Social Security number of the employee no later than 20 days after the employee is hired. The report is made on a W-4 form, which is simply mailed to the office in charge of the directory. The State Directory of New Hires must enter the employee information in its database within 5 days after it is received.

No later than May 1, 1998, each state will be required to have a matching system in place through which the Social Security numbers in the State Directory of New Hires are compared to the Social Security numbers of those who are delinquent in their child support obligation. If the comparison reveals a match (meaning the person who owes support has recently gone to work for a new employer), the State Directory of New Hires must report it to the agency charged with collecting child support, along with the information about where the payor has gone to work.

All this sounds like a dream come true to a parent who has been trying to collect past-due child support. But it gets better. The new law also requires the state agency in charge of enforcing child support orders to transmit a notice to the payor's employer directing the employer to withhold an amount equal to the monthly child support obligation from the payor's wages. This transmittal must occur within two days of the information regarding a newly hired employee being entered into the State Directory of New Hires. The new law also requires the creation of a National Directory of New Hires.

Information entered into the new hire directories may also be made available for use in locating payors, establishing paternity, and enforcing and modifying child support orders. The new law also allows the agencies in charge of administering employment security and workers' compensation programs to have access to the new hire directories. This is important because income withholding is broader than you might typically think. Income includes workers' compensation payments, disability payments, and payments to a pension or retirement program. These additional sources of income, along with other types of assets, may be seized by child support collection agencies. In short, the 1996 Welfare Reform Act gives teeth to the child support collection process, and state collection agencies are very excited about their new collection tools. More information about the increased enforcement resources brought about by the new federal law is included in later chapters.

b. Payors who are self-employed

The location and collection tools described in the previous section certainly are helpful, but what if the payor is self-employed? Unfortunately, the answer is that many of the important tools created by the 1996 Welfare Reform Act will not be available to you. Don't let that deter you. With a little hard work and creativity, you may still be able to locate the payor's income sources and get support collected for your children. Indeed, you can at least take comfort in the fact that once you find the payor, your search is over. You don't have to begin a new search geared toward finding the payor's employer.

This chapter deals primarily with wage withholding, which is usually not available when dealing with a self-employed payor. Nevertheless, collection efforts against a self-employed payor which primarily deal with assets are, in a sense, collection of wages, so the subject will be addressed in this chapter.

When collecting child support from a self-employed payor, your first step after locating the payor will be to confirm that he or she is engaged in a certain line of work. If you were married or had a long-term relationship with the payor, you are probably well aware of the type of work he or she would be pursuing to earn a living. Verifying the payor's line of work may be as simple as driving by his or her house. If he or she was trained as a plumber and there is a van, with the name Payor's Plumbing painted on the door, parked in the driveway, you can safely guess this is the current occupation of the payor.

In less obvious cases, you may need to do some in-depth investigating. Try to do as much of this as possible by calling friends and relatives who may know what the payor is doing to earn a living. If these attempts fail, you will probably need to hire a private investigator to follow the payor and discover his or her source of income based on whom he or she is associating with. Try not to stake out the payor yourself, or follow the payor around in hopes of finding out his or her income source. This type of conduct can lead to serious, or even violent, domestic disputes. There may be times, though, when you can do some investigating on your own and, in fact, have no other choice because you can't afford to hire a professional. If so, use discretion and don't let your investigating become an obsession.

c. Play your best cards

Many people who try to collect child support from a self-employed payor play the wrong cards. They try to collect by garnishing money owed to the payor by the payor's clients or customers. This is a difficult way to collect child support, because it is difficult to find out who owes money to the payor. It does have one advantage in that it gives you some leverage, because the payor may not want customers to know that he or she is behind on child support. Consequently, just the threat of garnishment may scare a delinquent self-employed payor into making payments.

A better collection strategy when dealing with a self-employed payor is to take a broad approach. You should not only garnish but also make an effort to discover the payor's assets and then take action to have them sold to satisfy past-due child support. (See chapter 5 for a detailed description of property liens.) The reason that property liens are so effective when collecting from self-employed payors is that these people often purchase business-related property with their earnings in order to expand their business. Sometimes, these business-related assets are exempt from sale to satisfy a debt, but the exemption is limited in many states to a specified dollar amount that is easily exceeded if the payor is successful in business.

Liens may be placed on either real estate or personal property. One good thing about a lien is that the payor cannot usually sell the property if it is subject to a lien. In other words, if the payor wants to sell his or her house, the payor will have to pay off your child support lien before doing so. Another good strategy when dealing with a self-employed payor is to locate a bank account and garnish it. Your local child support enforcement agency caseworker may be able to assist you in locating bank accounts.

One child support collection technique that is less likely to bear any fruit when dealing with a self-employed payor is an interception of tax refund money (see chapter 7). The reason is that self-employed payors rarely receive tax refunds. They typically make quarterly estimated tax payments that do not cover their actual tax burdens, which means that they usually owe taxes at the end of the year, rather than receive refunds.

Most child support enforcement workers will tell you that self-employed parents are the most difficult to collect child support from. This is puzzling, given that they have the most to lose by failing to pay child support. Their failure to pay can ultimately destroy their businesses or their good reputations. If you are trying to collect from a self-employed payor, make sure that he or she knows of these risks. But when you make your point, try to subtly emphasize the consequences of failing to pay, rather than lashing out at him or her.

Often, using a messenger can be effective. For example, you could tell the payor's business partner, or perhaps an employee, that you had been to the local child support enforcement agency and were surprised to learn how many tools that office had to collect child support, such as garnishments, liens, tax intercepts, and obtaining credit reports. You could add that you heard business-owners who fail to pay child support may have a hard time getting a loan because the unpaid child support shows up on a credit report. Finally, you could end the conversation by saying that you don't want anything like that to happen to your ex, but money is tight and you cannot make ends meet much longer.

Whether the payor is self-employed or employed at a job paying regular wages, it will be very important to continually keep track of the extent of the payor's earnings. As you will see in chapter 10, if the payor's wages increase, you may be able to increase child support payments. As long as the payor continues to earn income and you know his or her location, you should be able to collect child support. But if payments are not made, and wage withholding or other collection methods don't work, more forceful action may be necessary. The next chapter describes some more forceful techniques for collecting child support.

4

License revocation
— a new road

a. Lost without a license

Traveling a new road can leave you with mixed feelings —
exhilaration about the new scenery coupled with uncertainty
about what lies around the next corner. The same can be said
of the recent move toward license revocation as a means of
collecting child support.

Licenses have become an indispensable part of our lives.
Have you ever stopped to think about how difficult your life
would be if you had no driver's license? You couldn't drive
to work, to the store, or to visit friends and relatives. What if
you lost your license to work in your chosen profession? You
would have to find a new line of work, possibly at a much
lower wage.

Suppose you could not obtain a passport. If you needed to travel abroad for work or pleasure, you could not go. What if you wanted to go fishing or hunting, but could not get a license to do so? You would have to find another form of entertainment.

The government controls our ability to engage in many important activities by granting licenses to qualified people. And what the government gives, it may also take away. License revocation as a means of punishing people or convincing them to change their behavior is nothing new. For many years, states have suspended or revoked the driver's licenses of drunk drivers. People who hold professional licenses have been subject to loss of their license for misconduct or failure to pay annual licensing fees.

Recently, congress came to the realization that one way to encourage parents to pay child support is to revoke the driver's licenses, professional licenses, recreational licenses, and passports of parents who fail to pay. Hoping to increase child support collections and thereby lessen the burden of welfare on taxpayers, congress included license revocation requirements in the 1996 Welfare Reform Act. Under that act, states must pass laws that provide for the revocation of the licenses of parents who fail to pay child support. The U.S. Secretary of State also must refuse to issue a passport, or must revoke the passport, of a person who is certified by a state agency to have past-due child support exceeding $5,000.

Some states have already passed legislation allowing the suspension of licenses of parents who have failed to pay child support. For example, South Carolina recently enacted a license revocation law and, as a result, almost $1 million in past-due child support has been collected. In Florida, more than 6,000 payors were notified in 1995 that their driver's licenses would be suspended if they failed to pay their child support. When license revocation went into effect in Louisiana, many parents who owed past-due child support voluntarily contacted child support enforcement agencies so that they could avoid having their licenses revoked. All states must have license revocation laws in place by October 1, 1998, or they will lose millions of dollars in federal funding.

Typically, a state agency is in charge of revoking the license of a person who has failed to pay child support. Many states stipulate a certain dollar amount that must be owed, or a time period of delinquency that must be met, before license revocation proceedings may be filed. Usually, some sort of notice is given to the payor that action will be taken against his or her license unless child support is paid within a certain period. Some states provide the payor with a temporary license that is good for a few months but terminates unless child support is paid. Each state has different license revocation procedures, so you should check with your child support caseworker, or the agency in charge of issuing the license, to find out which procedures apply in your case.

There are several things to consider when trying to have a payor's license revoked for nonpayment of child support. At this point, it is not clear how most state license revocation laws will be implemented. Revocation may be automatic, but it may be difficult for states to set up procedures that provide proper notice to the agencies in charge of revoking licenses. Therefore, you should become familiar with the various licensing laws of your state so that you can take matters into your own hands, if necessary. The following summaries may be helpful.

1. Driver's license

All states have a Department of Motor Vehicles (DMV) or similar agency that takes care of matters related to driver's licenses. The DMV keeps track of things such as who has a driver's license and who is in danger of losing a driver's license due to traffic violations; it also administers the testing programs that enable a person to obtain a driver's license.

If you are owed child support and feel that the payor's driver's license should be revoked to encourage payment, you should contact your state's DMV. It should not be difficult to locate the proper person within the DMV to report the payor's delinquency. Just call the main DMV telephone number and ask to be connected to the department in charge of revoking the licenses of those who fail to pay child support.

You should be prepared to provide the DMV with information such as the payor's name, date of birth, and Social Security number. You should also be prepared to provide information about your child support order, such as the court in which it was entered, the date it was entered, the amount of unpaid support, and the name and telephone number of your child support caseworker, if any.

2. Professional license

As noted earlier, certain professions require a license. Lawyers, barbers, nurses, real estate agents, teachers, and many other professionals cannot earn a living in their field unless they hold a valid license or certificate granting them the right to practice. Unfortunately, professional licenses are much less common among child support payors than driver's licenses. However, if your payor has a professional license, you can use it as a powerful tool in your child support collection efforts. The holder of a professional license has likely spent a great deal of time, effort, and money to obtain that license and will often do whatever is necessary to hold onto it. If paying past-due child support is necessary to continue to earn a living, most people will make the payment required.

Arranging to have a professional license revoked will likely be very similar to the procedure involved with having a driver's license revoked. You should begin by notifying a child support agency caseworker of the past-due support and that the payor holds a professional license. If possible, obtain details of the license, such as the address and telephone number of the agency that issued the license, the date the license was issued, the type of license, and other identifying information, such as the payor's date of birth and Social Security number. You should provide this information to the child support collection caseworker.

It would also be a good idea to contact the licensing agency and determine whether there is a specific person within the agency to contact about license revocation for failure to pay child support. Once you learn that person's identity, you should contact him or her and provide as much information about the payor and the payor's license as possible.

If you, or the child support collection agency, take action to revoke the payor's professional license, be prepared to get some variation of the following complaint from the payor: You want me to pay child support, but how am I supposed to make payments if you take away the only means I have to earn a living? This, of course, is a very good question, and you might want to be prepared to respond with a sensible and logical response, although you do not have to provide any response at all. Unpaid child support is a serious matter, and payors who fail to provide that support have only themselves to blame.

Feel free to ignore the payor's complaints. On the other hand, if you want to respond, try simply pointing out that you understand that this is a drastic step, and that it's a step that you would have preferred not to take, but that you are in dire need of the support and that your children have been suffering because there are many things they need that you have not been able to afford. Consider leaving the door open to settlement at this point. After all, you do want the payor to earn a good living so that full payment can ultimately be made. You could agree to arrangements that assure regular payments of the court-ordered monthly support, together with an additional portion to be paid each month and applied toward the amount owed. That way, the payor gets back to work, child support payments are made, and you have hopefully gotten the payor's attention.

3. Recreational license

Recreational licenses may also be revoked for failure to pay child support. You might think that revocation of recreational licenses is not a very powerful child support enforcement tool. But in some cases it may work better than revocation of a driver's license or professional license.

To understand why, you must first realize that for some people the right to hunt, fish, and enjoy the great outdoors means more than the right to drive a car or work at a particular occupation. For these people, the revocation of a driver's license or professional license prevents them from doing things that are not all that enjoyable, like fighting traffic and dealing with a stressful job. Revocation of a recreational license, on the other hand, prevents them from doing the things they very much enjoy doing.

One reason that revocation of a recreational license is effective for a man who is in arrears in child support is that it prevents him from taking part in a traditional male bonding ritual. It is common for men to get together in groups to go out on hunting or fishing trips. For many men, the occasional hunting or fishing trip with their buddies is their most enjoyable social event. The thought of not being able to go on the annual hunting and fishing trip may be enough to convince a payor to clear up the balance of past-due child support. It can also be quite embarrassing if the guys discover that the reason Joe couldn't come on the hunting trip this year was that he hadn't paid his child support.

Recreational license revocation is also effective because it is directed at a segment of the population that is likely to owe child support, since nearly all hunters and fishers are men, and many more men pay child support than women.

36

According to the Federal Office of Child Support Enforcement, 85% of custodial parents are women and 15% are men.

Once again, if your payor is a hunter or a fisher, make certain that your child support agency caseworker knows about this and takes steps to either revoke the payor's recreational license or prevents him or her from getting one. If you want to take matters into your own hands, call your state's fish and game commission and ask for information about revocation of recreational licenses for failure to pay child support.

4. Passports

A passport is a lot like a license. In a sense, it is a license to travel the world. If your payor has to leave the United States for business, or has plans to take a vacation abroad, revocation of his or her passport may force payment of past-due child support.

You may also be owed child support by a person who has family abroad or who would like to return to his or her native country to live or visit. The new federal child support enforcement law will prevent the payor from leaving the country. The payor will have to postpone his or her business or pleasure trips until the child support has been paid.

The U.S. Secretary of State is responsible for issuing passports. The new federal law requires state agencies to certify to the Secretary of State that a payor owes child support in excess of $5,000. When this is done, the Secretary of State must refuse to issue a passport to the payor and may revoke or limit the passport of a payor who already possesses a passport. You should contact the child support enforcement agency, or directly contact the U.S. Secretary of State, to inquire about action against the passport of a payor who has failed to pay child support.

5. Other licenses

Federal law mandated states to enact laws providing for the revocation of driver's licenses, professional licenses, and recreational licenses. Many states have gone even further than what the federal law required. For example, the State of California may revoke or deny a commercial fisher's license to anyone who is delinquent in paying child support.

Cities have also taken up the child support collection torch. In Chicago, taxi drivers cannot receive the medallions that they need to do business if they are delinquent in their child support payments. In fact, if a taxi driver is delinquent in his or her child support payments, the city may sell the medallion (which is worth approximately $40,000) at auction and have the proceeds paid to the person entitled to receive the support. The City of Chicago also has the power to delay issuing licenses, contracts, loans, and employment to people who are delinquent in their child support payments.

b. Payor's right to appeal

At this point, it is too early to tell what type of procedures will be put into effect for those who owe child support to challenge the revocation of their licenses. Some states will probably not provide for any type of appeal from an agency decision to revoke a license. Other states do have limited means of appeal. Rest assured, though, that this appeal process will not provide an easy way for the payor to regain a license. Proving that child support has gone unpaid is as easy as requesting a certified copy of court records showing the status of the payor's account. In all likelihood, nothing short of extreme hardship, your signature on a release form, or full payment of the past-due child support will enable the payor to regain a license once it is revoked.

Finally, keep in mind that many state child support enforcement agencies consider license revocation to be more of a deterrent than a useful tool in the collection process. The reason for this attitude is that an overworked agency may have the time and inclination to pursue license revocation only when other collection methods have failed. Consequently, you may want to attempt to complete the revocation process yourself, if possible, or make regular contact with your caseworker and demand license revocation.

5

The property lien — traveling a difficult road

a. Creating and enforcing property liens

So far, we've covered the basics of finding yourself and the payor on the child support collection map (see Appendix 2), and cruising the interstate (wage withholding orders). Now, it's time to travel down a more difficult road. This is the road to a property lien. Actually, there is nothing difficult about obtaining a property lien. The difficulty lies in locating property that could be subject to a lien and then taking steps to enforce the lien.

The collection methods previously discussed are useful for obtaining a stream of payments or twisting the payor's arm with the threat of a change in lifestyle. But if you are owed many thousands of dollars and suspect that the payor is in possession of very valuable property, you should be directing your efforts toward creating and enforcing a property lien. Doing this will enable you to have the payor's property sold to satisfy the child support obligation.

At this point, you may be wondering: what is a lien? If you looked up the word lien in a law dictionary, you would find a definition that would probably leave you more confused than enlightened. A better idea would be to look at the definition contained in some of the government-published child support enforcement handbooks. They define a lien as a claim on property to prevent sale or transfer until a debt is satisfied. In other words, once you obtain a lien on the payor's property, you are in the driver's seat. To obtain the full benefit that a lien provides, you need to know just how powerful a lien can be and how to make it work for you. The starting point, of course, is placing the lien on the property.

1. Real estate

It is easy to place a child support lien on property. In fact, you may already have a lien on the payor's property and not even know it. In many states unpaid child support automatically becomes a judgment against the payor the moment it becomes delinquent. Therefore, the amount of past-due child support owed to your children may already be a lien on the real estate the payor owns in the jurisdiction where the child support order is entered. In most cases, there are no additional filing requirements needed to cause a judgment to become a lien on real estate within the jurisdiction where the child support order was entered.

If the payor owns real estate outside the jurisdiction, you may be able to simply file a certified transcript of the child support judgment in the jurisdiction where the real estate is located in order to have a lien placed on it.

This type of lien is called a judgment lien. A judgment lien on real estate is a good type of lien to have, because once it is created, the real estate will usually not be sold until the child support debt is paid. This is because no one wants to buy, or lend money to buy, real estate that is subject to a child support lien. Therefore, if the payor wants to sell his or her house, or other real estate, arrangements to pay past-due child support will have to be made in order to complete the sale.

Be aware that if you have a child support lien on the payor's real estate and he or she is trying to sell it, you may be asked to sign some legal paperwork that releases the lien and transfers it to other property the payor owns, or will own. Get advice from a lawyer before you sign anything of this nature. There really is no good reason to release and transfer a child support lien. Again, when you have the lien you are in a favorable position because without a release, the payor usually must pay the past-due child support in order to sell the property. Stand firm and you will probably be paid.

Section **2.** below discusses the fraudulent transfer of real estate.

2. Personal property

The payor's personal property may also be sold or seized to satisfy your child support judgment. Personal property is any property the payor owns that is not real estate, such as vehicles, boats, appliances, computers, stereo equipment, money, stock, and bank accounts. When you arrange to have personal property sold to satisfy a judgment, you are not really collecting on a lien. A judgment is usually not a lien on the debtor's personal property. This means that, unlike real estate, the payor may sell personal property and the property cannot be pursued once it is in the hands of the purchaser. As you might have suspected, this means that payors often fraudulently transfer their personal property to friends or relatives in an attempt to avoid having it sold to satisfy your child support judgment.

If you suspect that this has happened in your case, you should contact a lawyer and discuss the possibility of having these fraudulent transfers set aside. That is, consider having the transfer nullified so that the property goes back into the hands of the payor and is subject to your collection efforts. Real estate is also sometimes fraudulently transferred, and these transfers may also be set aside.

Some state child support enforcement laws allow an agency official to issue an order to withhold and deliver the payor's personal property. This order is sent to the person holding the property, such as a bank official when the property is a bank account or anyone else who may be holding the payor's personal property. The property must then be delivered to the agency for sale or delivery to the parent who is owed support.

When you become aware that the payor has property that could be sold to satisfy, or partially satisfy, your child support judgment, don't let the payor know that you are aware of the property's existence. And by all means, don't let the payor know that you intend to have the property seized and sold to satisfy your judgment. If you do, you run the risk that the payor will get rid of the property or hide it.

What if you learn that the payor is about to purchase expensive property, such as a new car, boat, or other big-ticket item? If the past-due child support you are owed exceeds $1,000, your child support enforcement office must report the debt to a credit reporting agency that requests information about it. Even if the credit reporting agency does not request information about the debt, some enforcement agencies will report it anyway. Contact your agency and ask to have your past-due child support reported to a credit agency. This may cause the payor to have to pay the past-due child support in order to get financing to make a big-ticket purchase.

The risk you run when you do this, however, is that the payor will simply decide not to make the purchase. You might be better off if the payor is able to make the purchase, because at least you could then seize the property, have it sold, and receive the amount left over after the loan against it is paid off.

Seizing and selling property is one area that you should thoroughly explore with your local child support enforcement agent. The new federal law places more power in the hands of state child support enforcement agencies, and they will be able to do many things that previously could be done only by the courts.

b. Who benefits from a lien?

Not everyone who has a child support lien on property will necessarily benefit from it. Sometimes, the property subject to the lien, such as a house or car, is already subject to another lien, such as a lien a bank placed on the property when it loaned the payor the money to purchase it. If the other lien is in an amount that equals, or nearly equals, the value of the property, you may not receive any money if the property is sold. In fact, you may not even be able to have the property sold. This is because most state laws provide that a debtor may retain a certain level of property as exempt from sale by those to whom he owes money. For example, in Nebraska, the first $10,000 in equity in a debtor's home is exempt. This means that there is no use in attempting to have a payor's home sold unless the payor has more than $10,000 in equity in it. Equity is the dollar difference between the value of the property and the loan or lien against it.

Keep in mind that a child support lien may be more effective if you act quickly. This is because a delay in creating the lien may enable other people who have loaned money to the payor, or who have judgments against the payor, to get priority over your lien because theirs were created before yours. The lesson here is to take steps to impose the lien on property as soon as it can legally be done. If you are at all uncertain about the steps necessary to create a lien, contact a lawyer.

c. Getting an advance lien

With a little foresight, and a lot of luck, you may be able to entirely avoid problems with collecting child support. The way to do this is to plan, before the entry of the initial child support order, for the possibility that support won't be paid. If you can show the judge that there is some uncertainty about payment and that reasonable arrangements may be made to guarantee payment, you may be able to arrange what is essentially an advance lien.

One type of advance lien is a bond. You may be able to convince the judge to order the payor to post a bond, just as a construction contractor is required to do to guarantee his or her performance. In other words, the bonding company is insuring the payment of child support. If the payor fails to pay child support, the bonding company must pay.

Another possibility is to ask the judge to order the payor to purchase life insurance and name your children as beneficiaries so that if the payor dies, your children will receive money to replace the support they would have received had the payor lived.

Yet another way to guarantee payment is to request a court order establishing a trust fund. The judge may appoint a trustee to take control of certain assets that are to be managed, with the income or principal from that fund being used to support the children.

d. Liens as locators

Liens are not only useful as direct collection devices, they are also useful tools for locating the payor and his or her property. Most states have a central location where personal property liens are recorded. This office is usually located in the Uniform Commercial Code (UCC) division of the Secretary of State. You may request a UCC search to determine whether a certain person has any property subject to a lien. There are millions of UCC financing statements filed every year so that lenders may have enforceable liens against property, typically motor vehicles.

Another good source for locating a payor is the county assessor's office in the county where the payor owns real estate. Just call the assessor's office and ask whether the payor owns any property in the county. The assessor should be able to tell you the value of any property the payor owns in the county. You can then get information from the county register of deeds about mortgages against the property, and with this information you may be able to determine whether the payor has any equity in the property. That is, whether the value of the property exceeds the amount of the loan against it.

e. A final note about liens

You will probably find that pursuing a lien will either leave you frustrated and wishing you had never wasted your time with it, or thrilled at the large recovery you receive. The key is to do plenty of homework before deciding to pursue a lien to collect child support from the payor.

6

Computer as travel guide

a. A powerful collection tool

Some trips require more than a map. They require a travel guide who can accompany you every step of the way and give you information that not only makes the trip easier but also more enjoyable. A computer can be an excellent travel guide as you follow your child support collection map (see Appendix 2).

By now, you've probably figured out that computers are a very useful tool for tracking down parents who owe child support and collecting money from them. You don't have to be very knowledgeable about computers to take advantage of them in your child support collection efforts. In fact, a lot of the actual computer work is done for you by agency case workers and other people. Nevertheless, you can benefit greatly from a full understanding of the many and varied uses of computers in the child support collection process.

The most common uses of computers in the child support collection process are for locating the payor, locating the payor's place of employment, and locating the payor's assets. In addition to these uses, computers can aid in learning about the child support collection process and the management of collection data. These are broad categories, but within each category there are numerous variations in the way a computer can be used.

We have already addressed how to locate a payor (see chapter 2). However, our previous discussion did not contain many of the details that are worth knowing about the use of a computer to locate a payor.

In pre-computer days, locating a person who owed child support involved a lot of legwork, telephone calls, and time-consuming manual searches of official records. That has changed dramatically as government and private records have been placed into computer databases, and child support enforcement agents have been given the power to search those records. Computer location can generally be placed into two categories — location you can perform on your own computer, and location authorized people do on your behalf. The computer tools you use will primarily involve using the Internet.

b. Getting on the Internet

Any discussion of the computer location methods that you can do on your own must start with the Internet. The Internet is a global network of computers which is accessed through an ordinary telephone line. Many people are already thoroughly familiar with the Internet, its power, and how to use it for their benefit. If you fall into that category, the following information may at times be too basic for you. Nevertheless, you could also find some very useful information, so read on, even if you consider yourself an expert.

Let's first assume that you do not own a computer, know nothing about them, and know less about the Internet. Gaining access to a computer will be your first task.

You may be one of the thousands of people who have always thought about purchasing a computer but have just never got around to buying one. Now may be the time to jump in and make the purchase. Computers are not as difficult to operate as you might think, and you don't really need to know how the computer works. All you need to know is that it does work and is very useful. Today's software is much more user-friendly than previous versions and literally walks you through the steps necessary to learn how to operate the computer. The point is, if the only reason you have been putting off buying a computer is because you don't think you can learn how to operate it, put that concern aside. If five-year-old children can operate a computer, you surely can, too.

Cost might be a concern, and understandably so. The low-end price for a new computer is in the neighborhood of $1,500, and you can spend as much as $5,000 if you get a high-end model. Fortunately, cost should not be a barrier to your ability to take advantage of computer technology in your child support collection efforts. The explosion in home-computer use has caused a glut of available used computers. You may be able to find a good used computer for about half of what you would pay for a new one. A used computer will not have the power (speed, disk storage space, etc.) of a new one, but for your purposes, you don't really need a high-powered computer. Be sure to ask a knowledgeable friend to help you look at computers and help you determine if an Internet accessible model (new or used) is within your budget.

For those who must be even more cost-conscious, there is another alternative. Most public libraries now have computers available for public use. Many of these computers are hooked up to the Internet. The nice thing about public library computers is that not only do you not have to pay anything to use them but there is usually a librarian nearby who has knowledge about accessing and searching the Internet.

As you consider whether to purchase a computer to help with your child support collection activities, think about all the other uses it would have. Your children are probably already using a computer if they are in school and would benefit from being able to use one at home. You could keep track of family finances, prepare your tax returns, write letters, make greeting cards, and enjoy countless other aspects of home computing. You can also use the Internet for other tasks besides child support collection, such as keeping in touch with friends and relatives, following current events, conducting research, and gathering information on your favorite activity or hobby. If this sounds like a sales pitch for a computer company, you have my apology, but you really are putting yourself and your children at a disadvantage by avoiding using a computer.

Another option that is available for people who do not want to purchase a computer or learn how to use one is to begin asking friends and relatives whether they have access to the Internet. After you find an Internet user, ask for help in searching for the payor, the payor's assets, place of employment, and other details. Many people who use the Internet are eager to teach others how to use it or use their own skills to benefit another person.

To gain access to the Internet after you have purchased a computer, you will need to sign up with an Internet service provider. Many people obtain Internet access through commercial on-line companies such as America Online, CompuServe, and the Microsoft Network. The commercial on-line companies are a good choice for a beginner, but costs can vary greatly, so make sure you get the details about monthly fees and the amount of access time available for that fee, before you sign up.

Local Internet service providers are also a good option. These local companies are springing up all over the country, so you should be able to find a local company to provide you with access. Perhaps even your local telephone company offers Internet access.

Some people are lucky enough to gain Internet access through their employers. If you fall into this category, find out about your employer's rules on using its Internet connection for personal use before taking advantage of it.

c. Putting the Internet to work

Getting connected to the Internet is the hard part. The fun begins once you are on-line. The first thing you will want to do is get familiar with a search directory; it will enable you to type in search words that direct you to pages on the World Wide Web (WWW), also referred to as Web pages. A Web page is simply a computer site, set up by a person or company, that contains information along with links to other related Web pages. The Internet is much more than just a collection of Web pages, but for our purposes, a discussion about Web pages will provide you with most of the information you need to make the Internet useful in your child support collection efforts.

The Internet terms discussed so far may seem strange if you have no Internet experience, but be assured that there is not much more in the way of terminology that you must learn in order to make meaningful use of the Internet. This is a simplified explanation of Internet usage, so be prepared to learn more about it as you experiment with it. Indeed, as with many other computer issues, just getting on the Internet and experimenting is probably the best way to learn how to use it.

For child support collection purposes, the Internet's resources may generally be divided into the categories discussed in the sections below.

Please note that the Web sites listed below do not contain references to the Internet addresses for each site, such as www.self-counsel.com. The reason is that these sites may all be accessed by typing their names into one of the listed search directories, or by following a link set up from another source. Most people do not manually type in the address of a Web site to access it.

1. Search directories

One of the easiest ways to search the Internet is to type keywords into a search directory. A keyword is simply a word that relates to your topic of interest. If you wanted to find information on child support, you could access one of the search directories listed below; type in "child support," and wait for the computer to give you its search results. After a few seconds, the computer will provide you with a list of resources related to child support. Search directories can be very useful in many areas of child support collection because they can connect you to services that locate people, provide you with access to public records, educate you about child support collection procedures, and link you to other people who can help with your collection efforts. Try the following search directories:

- Albert2
- AltaVista
- The Argus Clearinghouse
- A2Z
- Excite
- IBM Infomarket
- Infoseek
- G.O.D.
- LookSmart
- Lycos

- Nerd World Media
- 100 Hot Websites
- Point
- Webcrawler
- What's New
- Yahoo!

Your Internet service provider will likely have links to many of these search directories on its home page, which is the page that initially comes up on your screen when you log onto the Internet. All you need to do is gain access to a search directory, and from there, type in the name of any of the above search directories to obtain a link to it. Experiment with several different search directories until you find the one that you like best.

2. Locators and notifiers

Search directories provide the means for finding useful Internet sites. If you cannot locate your payor, one way to search for him or her is to connect to an Internet locator service. These services can provide names, addresses, telephone numbers, and e-mail addresses for millions of people. Most of them are nothing more than a huge database of telephone book information. The nice thing about the locator services is that they will almost certainly locate the payor if he or she has a listed telephone number. All you need to do is type in the payor's name.

One of the best locator services is LookupUSA, through American Business Information. This company has a huge database containing millions of telephone records and data from other public records. It enables you to conduct name searches based on geographical areas of the United States. For example, if you think your payor lives in the northeast United States, you can simply access the database for the northeast region and type in the payor's name. If the payor has a listed telephone number in that area of the country, chances are his or her name and address will appear on your computer screen.

An added advantage provided by the LookupUSA service is that it also contains business records. This can be very helpful if you are looking for a self-employed payor. This type of payor may have an unlisted residential telephone number, but it's a safe bet that his or her business number will not be unlisted. At least it won't be unlisted if the payor is in business to make money.

Other useful locator services include:

- BigBook
- Bigfoot
- BigYellow
- 411Locate
- GTESuperpages
- Homepages@WhoWhere?
- OnlineCompanies@WhoWhere?
- On'Village
- Zip2

3. Public and private records

Public records, such as government agency databases, are not yet very accessible through the Internet. This is slowly changing, and someday you may be able to access just as much information from your computer as from the local courthouse or government agency office. But we are dealing with what is available now, and that means you will probably be limited to searching personal property liens (Uniform Commercial Code records). If a lien search is available, there may be a charge associated with it. To find out which public record searches are available in the area in which you suspect your payor lives, conduct a search for the state and local government Web pages in that area.

Private records, such as cable television, utility, and employment records are not accessible through the Internet. Your child support agency caseworker, however, should have access to many private databases. This subject is addressed more fully later in this chapter.

4. Agency links

Child support enforcement agencies in many states now have Web pages that are useful in many ways. They provide information about the child support collection process — a means of contacting agencies and caseworkers — and provide a forum where you may post information about your payor. Your child support caseworker should be able to tell you whether your state or county has a Web page and, if so, how to access it.

If the Web page in your jurisdiction has a Most Wanted feature, consider taking advantage of it for locating the payor. This feature is a forum for posting information about the Most Wanted parents who have failed to pay child support and cannot be located. It contains information about an absent parent, such as the parent's photograph, last known address, the amount of child support owed, and other identifying facts. Not only do many state and local child support agencies have a Most Wanted feature, but there are also many privately operated Web pages that offer this same feature. Typically, these other Web pages are sponsored by private child support collection agencies or people who have taken up the cause of child support collection. Anyone who is having difficulty locating a payor would do well to contact these Web page operators and provide information about their payor so that it may be posted for others to view.

The following Web sites are operated by child support collection agencies, private child support collection companies, and private individuals. This list is a sampling only. Web sites are changing and being created all the time. Be sure to search for a Web site for your state's agency if it's not listed below.

- Federal Office of Child Support Enforcement
- California Child Support Enforcement
- Connecticut Child Support Enforcement (Most Wanted Page)
- Florida Child Support Enforcement
- Hawaii Child Support Enforcement
- Indiana Child Support Enforcement (Most Wanted Page)
- Iowa Child Support Enforcement
- Massachusetts Child Support Enforcement
- New York Child Support Enforcement
- Texas Child Support Enforcement (Most Wanted Page)
- Washington Child Support Enforcement
- Childhelp.com
- Child Support Advocacy Network
- Child Support Network (Family Law Adviser)
- Child Support Reform Initiative
- Deadbeat Victims' Voice
- Domestic Relations Association of Pennsylvania
- Single Parents Association
- Yahoo! — Commercial Collection Agencies

The Federal Office of Child Support Enforcement Web page is a very good resource. It provides you with access to the computer file version of the *Child Support Enforcement Handbook*. It also provides links to state agencies and is a means of accessing the child support laws in each of the 50 states plus Guam and Puerto Rico. The Yahoo! listing of child support collection sites is also a good resource.

As you might expect, not all the child support-related Web sites on the Internet are geared toward providing assistance to people who are owed child support. There are also many Web sites for people who pay child support and are unhappy with the way the system is administered. These include the Men's Issues Page in the Virtual Law Library, Child Support USA, Divorcenet.com, and END (www.smart-net.net). Take a look at these Web pages and read some of the concerns posted by parents who are paying child support. It can be a real eye-opener and will definitely give you a view from the other side of the fence.

5. Usenet — networking with others

It's nice to be able to access a Web page and read information about the child support collection process. But what if you have a question that is not answered by the general information provided by the Web page? That's where the interactive nature of the Internet comes in handy. The Internet provides a worldwide bulletin board system for people who want to post a message within a particular newsgroup. This bulletin board system is accessed through the Usenet service. There is a Usenet newsgroup that specifically addresses child support issues. Perhaps the easiest way to access this huge discussion group is to find your way onto the newsgroup area of one of the following services:

- AltaVista

- Dejanews

- Divorce.net (Child Support Network)

- Excite

- Infoseek

- reference.com

- The Usenet Newsstand

Once you gain access to the newsgroup, you need only post your message and await a reply by someone who reads it. The reply will come by e-mail from the person or persons who decide to respond. You can even sign up for a mailing list on the topic of child support that enables you to automatically receive regular e-mail messages discussing child support issues. Reference.com has a directory of mailing lists, including names, descriptions, and subscription information. You can use this directory to find the child support mailing lists.

d. Computers behind the scenes

Even if you do not use a computer yourself to assist with the child support collection process, you can greatly benefit from the computer work of people working behind the scenes — most notably, child support agency caseworkers. The newly enacted federal law places great emphasis on computer-based collection techniques. Your caseworker should have access to an abundance of records, both public and private.

Recall from earlier in the book that employers are now required to report the names of newly hired employees to the government for placement in a database that may be used by child support collection agents. These records are regularly compared with child support agency records so that delinquent payors may be located and their employment identified. This is a computer-conducted comparison, which makes it quick and efficient.

In addition, child support caseworkers have access to private records, such as utility records, cable television records, and credit reports, which are typically kept in company computer databases.

Because of this expanded and powerful computer access, you should make every effort to stay in touch with your caseworker and request specific computer-related location searches. Let your caseworker know that you are aware of his or her broad powers of access to computer records, and that you want all possible records searched on your behalf. If your caseworker knows that you are aware of the tools at his or her disposal, he or she will more likely use those tools rather than having to admit that an avenue has gone unexplored. This is especially true if you call periodically to ask whether a particular type of computer search has been conducted.

7

Intercepting an income tax refund

a. Leave the driving to the government

Some trips are more enjoyable if you leave the driving to someone else. Take a bus or a plane and you don't have to worry about what a map says. Someone else reads the map for you and gets you to your destination. One way to have someone else do the work necessary to collect child support is to request interception of the payor's tax refund money. All you need to do is make the request to the right agency and the government will do the collection work for you.

Ben Franklin said that "in this world nothing is certain but death and taxes." The federal government is well aware of this certainty, and that is one reason why congress granted child support collection agencies the power to intercept the tax refunds of parents who owe child support. Interception of tax refunds for nonpayment of child support is not a complicated subject. In fact, you may have already surmised this from the length of this chapter. There really is not a lot to discuss once you learn a few basic concepts.

b. Tax refund interception basics

The program that was established to intercept the tax refunds of parents who owe past-due child support is technically referred to as the Federal Tax Refund Offset Program. You might want to think of the tax refund collection process as an interception program, rather than an offset program. An interception sounds more daring and proactive than a dull, lifeless offset. If you are able to tell someone that you intercepted a tax refund, you will feel that you have actually accomplished something, rather than just having the past-due child support offset against the payor's tax refund. Why not characterize it as an accomplishment?

The tax refund interception program is administered by the IRS, the Federal Office of Child Support Enforcement, and the State Child Support Enforcement agencies. The program has been a very effective means of collecting past-due child support. Since 1982, more than $6 billion in past-due child support has been collected through this program. The average tax refund offset in 1995 was $721. In December of 1996 alone, there were 15,412 tax refund offsets for a total amount of more than $9 million.

c. How to participate in the tax refund interception program

To be eligible for the program, you must be owed delinquent child support. Child support is considered delinquent for purposes of the interception program if the payor is three months behind in child support payments. There is also a threshold amount of child support that must be owed before you can take advantage of the program. If you receive Aid to Families with Dependent Children (AFDC) payments, you must be owed at least $150 in delinquent child support before the payor's tax refund may be intercepted. If you do not receive AFDC payments, the threshold amount is $500. One of the benefits of tax refund interception is that it is not limited by state boundaries. A tax refund may be intercepted to pay past-due child support no matter where in the United States the payor lives.

If you meet the threshold requirements, it is easy to get your case submitted for participation in the tax refund interception program. You need only contact a child support enforcement agency caseworker and make certain that the agency has the payor's name and Social Security number, and knows the amount of past-due support owed. The agency is required to submit all cases, both AFDC and non-AFDC to the IRS. If you know the payor's address, you should also provide it to the agency so that it can notify the payor of the pending tax refund interception. This notification is required.

Once the payor is notified he or she will have the right to challenge the interception by submitting evidence that the child support has been paid, or that an incorrect amount is shown as due. However, it is rare for a payor who challenges the interception to have the amount intercepted reduced or eliminated.

d. The mechanics of tax refund interception

Experience has probably taught you that when the government is involved, things do not happen overnight. This is especially true when you are dealing with a federal agency, the IRS, and a state agency. Therefore, you need to have patience when waiting for word on whether any money has been intercepted from the payor's tax refund. The IRS processes tax returns from February through December and simply determines whether the payor is owed a tax refund. If so, an amount of money equal to the past-due child support is taken out of the refund and sent to the Federal Office of Child Support Enforcement. This office then forwards the money to the state child support enforcement office.

In AFDC cases, the state will keep most, if not all, of the money to reimburse itself for the money it paid to you. In non-AFDC cases, the entire amount is paid to you. If you received AFDC in the past, but no longer receive it, the state will keep an amount necessary to repay itself for any AFDC you were paid. The remainder, if any, is then paid to you. Typically, it will take three to five weeks from the time the IRS processes the payor's tax return until your state receives the money. The state may hold the intercepted tax refund money for several months if it involves a non-AFDC case and a joint tax return.

Your state may charge a fee for processing a tax refund interception. This is especially true in non-AFDC cases. This fee cannot be more than $25.

The timing of a request for a tax refund interception is important. Remember that April 15 comes only once a year, so make certain that your caseworker has the necessary information well before that date. In fact, it is a good idea to inquire as to whether there is a deadline for making requests for a tax refund interception.

e. Interception strategy

Intercepting a tax refund is a great way to collect past-due child support. Its drawback, of course, is that many payors are either unemployed, or are employed and pay little or no taxes. You simply cannot intercept a tax refund if no tax refund is owed to the payor. Your best strategy, if you have a payor who is not paying taxes, is to try to get the payor into tax-paying status. This not only carries the benefit of a possible tax refund interception but also creates the likelihood of a wage withholding order.

If the payor is self-employed, you stand virtually no chance of collecting past-due child support through an interception of a tax refund. The reason for this is that a self-employed person usually makes estimated tax payments to the IRS every few months. These payments usually do not meet the payor's total tax burden for the year and the payor must then pay an amount to the IRS by April 15 to cover his or her entire tax obligation. In short, a self-employed person usually doesn't have a tax refund to intercept. Don't waste your time trying to intercept a tax refund if you have a self-employed payor. Your collection efforts are better directed toward other methods of obtaining payment.

Finally, if you suspect that the payor is employed, but no taxes are being withheld from his or her paycheck, consider reporting the employer to the IRS. Employers are required to withhold taxes and a failure to do so could subject them to civil or criminal penalties. Usually, if an employer fails to withhold taxes, it is because the payor and the employer are friends and the employer is doing the payor a favor by preventing the payment of taxes and a possible interception of a refund. Don't accept any explanations from the payor for the lack of tax withholding, such as, "I'm an independent contractor," or, "I'm exempt from withholding." The law applies equally to all employers, and if you suspect that your payor is being given a favor by an employer/friend, don't hesitate to go to the IRS and request that it check out the situation.

f. Intercepting lottery money

Have you ever suspected that your payor was spending money on frivolous things, such as lottery tickets, rather than child support payments? Take heart. If he or she ever hits the jackpot, there is a good chance that the winnings will first be applied to your past-due child support before the payor receives anything. This is because many states with lotteries now have a system in place through which they check whether anyone who is entitled to lottery money owes past-due child support. If he or she does, the lottery money is intercepted in a manner similar to a tax refund interception.

8

Paternity and the unmarried payor

a. A different starting point

We previously discussed how important it is to find your location on a map before beginning your trip to collect child support. There are two basic starting points for everyone: as a participant in a divorce case, or, as a participant in a paternity case. This chapter covers the second starting point — a paternity case. The child support collection map of a parent involved in a paternity case is not much different from that of a parent involved in a divorce case. Sometimes, the father in a paternity case can be a bit more difficult to locate and denies fathering the child. These are the two most significant differences, but several others are discussed below.

b. Presumptions and the law

There are many presumptions in life that are usually true. Usually, a child's parents are the best people to care for the child, rather than some unrelated person. Usually, it is best for a noncustodial parent to pay an amount of child support based on his or her income. Usually, when a man and a woman are married, a child born of the wife was fathered by the husband.

Since some things are usually true, the law has developed in such a way over the years to recognize presumptions that lessen the burden of proving certain facts. The law presumes that a natural parent is the best person to care for a child. The law presumes that child support payments should be set at a level based on income. The law presumes that a child born of a husband and wife was fathered by the husband.

These presumptions are often called rebuttable presumptions because the person against whom the presumption is directed can come into court and rebut it. That is, he or she can attempt to prove that the facts are otherwise than as presumed. For example, a party (usually the state) claiming that a child should not live with his or her parents may prove that the parents are unfit because they abuse or neglect the child. A person who is ordered to pay child support based on his or her income can come into court and prove that it would be unfair to do so because, perhaps, he or she recently became disabled and will suffer a drastic drop in income.

An important legal presumption in the child support context is that a child born of married parents was fathered by the husband. It enables a court to enter a child support order at the time of a divorce without getting into the question of who actually fathered the child. As you might expect, the paternity presumption does not exist when parents are unmarried. That is, if parents are not married when a child is born, there is no presumption that a certain person is the father. Consequently, there will not be any child support due from the father if he leaves the family and fails to provide financial support unless steps are taken to legally prove the father is, in fact, the biological father of the child. The legal procedure used to prove that someone is the father of a child is called a paternity action. If you are seeking child support from a man to whom you were never married, and you believe that he is indeed the child's father, you must pursue a paternity action in order to get a court order establishing paternity.

If you are receiving public assistance payments, the state will file a paternity action for you. You need only provide a child support agency caseworker with identifying information about the child's father. In fact, mothers who receive AFDC are required to cooperate with child support collection agencies and identify the possible father of the child unless the mother has good cause not to identify the child. Good cause would exist if, for example, the alleged father has threatened to harm you and you do not want him to know your whereabouts.

If you do not receive public assistance payments, you may need to pursue the paternity case on your own. Do not delay in doing this. It is well worth the time, effort, and expense, and even though most states allow courts to order retroactive child support to the date of the child's birth, not all courts actually do this. The sooner you act to establish paternity, the sooner you will begin receiving payments.

c. Establishing paternity

The first step in establishing paternity is to locate and identify the father. If you are reasonably certain who the father is, but cannot locate him, use some of the techniques described in chapter 2. If you are receiving, or have received, public assistance and the state will be pursuing the paternity action,

71

the state child support collection agency will attempt to locate the father. Of course, even though the agency is obligated to search for the father, you will probably want to make your own location efforts to supplement the agency work. This will be especially important if the agency is overburdened, as most are, and cannot give sufficient attention to locating the father.

Whether proceeding through an agency or on your own, make certain that you and your caseworker have as much information as possible about the father. This would include the nature of your relationship with him, the timing of your pregnancy and birth of your child, whether the father has ever provided financial support for the child, and whether the father has ever admitted to being the child's father. An admission of paternity need not be a direct statement by the father that the child is his, but can be implied from such things as financial support, providing gifts to the child, and caring for the child.

In most states, a father can admit paternity by signing a document. A good way to get this done is to have the father present shortly after the child is born when documents related to the child, such as the birth certificate, newspaper announcement, and other legal papers are reviewed and signed. The person presenting the paperwork can include an acknowledgment of paternity form with the rest of the papers and ask the father to sign it. If the acknowledgment is presented in this manner, the father will be less likely to refuse to sign than if later presented with the acknowledgment form alone. Most fathers, when asked to sign official paperwork in front of the mother, new baby, family members, and hospital staff, will not raise a fuss about whether the child is really his unless there are solid grounds for denying paternity.

A paternity action is not prevented merely because a father refuses to acknowledge paternity in writing or otherwise. Since October of 1989, all parties in a contested paternity case are required to submit to genetic tests if the other party so requests. A genetic test is sometimes referred to as a blood test because the mother, child, and alleged father all have to provide blood samples. After the blood samples are provided, it takes four to eight weeks for the laboratory to return the test results. This type of test is very accurate and provides results with a 99% certainty that a man is the father of a child.

Genetic testing has become very routine in paternity cases and has drastically changed the manner in which these cases proceed. In the days before genetic testing, the mother had to come into court with evidence such as sexual relations at about the time the child was conceived, similarity in physical features between the alleged father and the child, and other evidence of paternity such as supporting the child or admitting paternity.

Today, most fathers involved in paternity cases do not even challenge the fact of paternity because they are aware of the highly accurate nature of the blood test. As a result, the primary issue in most paternity cases is what amount of child support should be paid and whether the father should also pay additional expenses, such as childbirth costs, health insurance, and daycare expenses.

d. Preparing for a paternity case

Before going into court in a paternity case, make certain that you are armed with all the information necessary to ensure that a fair child support order is entered. It is never too early to get started with the case. In fact, the paperwork can be started before the child is born. You will need to obtain copies of the father's tax returns, current wage stubs, and any other information related to his earning power. Your lawyer or the child support agency caseworker should do this. If he or she does not have this information, ask him or her to get it well in advance of the hearing.

In addition to this basic income information, you should obtain verification of the extent of the father's education, the type of job he is qualified to obtain, and other sources of income, such as investments or financial assistance from friends or family. One point to remember is that child support is not always based solely on a parent's recent earning record. If a parent has the potential to earn much more than he or she is currently earning, then the judge should set child support at a level that reflects the parent's earning capacity. In other words, if the father of your child is a medical doctor, but he has been working as a short-order cook for the past year, you should make the judge aware of this fact and ask that child support be set at the level typically paid by a doctor.

You will also be asked to provide your own income information. Do not hold anything back. If you expect the father to be totally forthcoming with all of his income information, you should do no less yourself. It would also be a good idea to provide your caseworker or lawyer with information about your monthly expenses, with an emphasis on health care expenses, daycare expenses, and any other expenses that are out of the ordinary.

e. Settlement agreements

Don't be surprised if your child's father, or his lawyer, presents you with a proposal to settle the child support issue by agreement. Be careful when entering into a settlement agreement. There is absolutely no reason for you to agree to payment of child support at a level below what your state's child support guidelines provide for the father's income level. Even if the proposed settlement includes a level of child support matching the father's reported income, remember that the reported income may be inaccurate or may not reflect the father's true earning capacity. Judges easily see through a father's attempt to understate his income or earning capacity. There is no reason to agree to a settlement if you think there is a chance that a judge would find that the father's earnings, or earning capacity, may be understated. You should also think twice about entering into a settlement agreement that does not include paying for childbirth expenses nor a clear statement as to who is responsible for providing health insurance and paying daycare expenses. Finally, it is a good idea to include a specific and detailed agreement as to the terms of visitation in any settlement agreement.

If you expect to engage in settlement negotiations with your child's father, it would be a good idea to hire a lawyer to assist you. After all, a child support order is in effect for many years. Just a slight increase in the amount of support that is ordered can pay for the lawyer's fee in a couple of years. For example, assume that you have to pay a lawyer $1,000 to negotiate a settlement agreement on your behalf. If the father is offering to pay $250 per month in support, and a lawyer is able to establish that $350 is a fair amount, your lawyer's fee will be paid in ten months.

It is also possible that the father will be ordered to pay all, or a portion, of your lawyer's fees. When hiring a lawyer, however, keep in mind that the additional amount that could be obtained doesn't mean much if the father never pays. In other words, if you are dealing with a father who definitely will never pay support, it may be a waste of money to hire a lawyer.

f. Benefits of establishing paternity

Some mothers think that it is not important to formally establish their child's paternity because they are on good terms with the father, have been misled into thinking that establishing paternity is not necessary, or don't think that the father could pay child support. Don't let these, or any other reasons, prevent you from pursuing a paternity action. There are many more benefits to establishing paternity than being able to receive child support. Consider the following benefits that are typically available to your children only if paternity is formally established:

(a) Inheritance rights to father's property

(b) Coverage under the father's medical insurance

(c) Life insurance benefits under the father's policy

(d) Social Security benefits through father

(e) Veterans' benefits through father

(f) Wrongful death benefits through father

(g) Access to father's family medical records that detail genetic diseases

(h) The emotional benefit to the child of knowing who both his or her parents are

In short, the benefits of establishing paternity are so great that only rarely is it a good idea not to do it.

g. Visitation

There was a time when unwed fathers had few rights to their children. However, during the last couple of decades, the U.S. Supreme Court has decided several cases that recognize the constitutional rights of unwed fathers to participate in the lives of their children. Today, all courts recognize that it is a good idea for fathers to visit their children. Therefore, it is likely that the judge in your case will include visitation rights for the father in your paternity order.

Don't consider the visitation order to be an imposition in your life. It is indeed a good thing for children to know their father and to have regular interaction with him. If you expect the father to pay child support and other expenses, you should be willing to allow him regular visitation. In fact, statistics show that you will be much more likely to actually receive child support payments from the father if you allow regular visitation.

If you are not on good terms with your children's father, don't let the problems between the two of you spill over into such an important area as visitation rights. Even if you do not receive child support payments, it is a good idea to continue to allow visitation. Denying visitation just gives a father another reason to fail, or continue to fail, to pay child support.

h. New agency power

Your state child support collection agency will soon have additional powers at its disposal in paternity cases. The 1996 Welfare Reform Act contains a mandate that states enact laws designed to make it easier to establish paternity. States must enact laws making genetic testing mandatory in paternity cases and allowing paternity cases to be filed at any time before the child reaches the age of 18 years. States must also pass laws creating hospital-based paternity establishment programs. In other words, hospitals will soon be required to present unwed parents with the paperwork necessary for voluntary acknowledgment of paternity either immediately before or after the child is born.

The state agency responsible for maintaining birth records must also have a voluntary paternity establishment program. States must also pass laws allowing an unmarried father's name to be included on birth records only if he and the mother voluntarily admit to paternity, and a court or administrative agency enters a paternity order. There must also be a procedure in place that makes a signed voluntary acknowledgment of paternity a binding legal document, subject to the father's right to rescind (withdraw) the acknowledgment. The father must rescind within 60 days after he signs the acknowledgment or before a paternity order is entered, whichever is earlier.

Perhaps one of the most important parts of the 1996 Welfare Reform Act as it relates to paternity proceedings is that it prohibits jury trials in paternity cases. This should speed up the paternity determination in many cases because it will eliminate the delay that is usually present when waiting for presentation of a case to a jury.

i. If you already have a paternity settlement agreement

Recent changes in the law have made it important for many mothers who entered into paternity settlement agreements to review the agreement for validity. The courts in many states have invalidated paternity settlement agreements that provided for a lump sum or locked-in payment to settle the paternity case. The reason is that mothers and children who entered into such settlement agreements were denied their constitutional right to equal protection under the law.

The constitutional violation is based on the fact that mothers of children born within a marriage cannot enter into an agreement that prevents a child from later modifying a child support obligation so that it is a fair payment. The courts now hold that mothers of children born out of wedlock should be entitled to the same protection. Therefore, if you entered into a paternity settlement agreement that prevents you from increasing child support payments or forced you to take a lump sum payment, you should see a lawyer immediately to get an opinion about the validity of the agreement.

9

Agency caseworkers: overworked tour guides

a. Too busy to help?

The government will provide you with a tour guide as you take your child support collection trip. These tour guides are the child support enforcement agency caseworkers whose job it is to help you collect child support. Unfortunately, these tour guides are essentially in charge of a 20-minute tour, with 200 people, and all of them are asking questions. It is simply impossible to answer 200 questions in 20 minutes. Some questions have to go unanswered. In other words, your caseworker/tour guide is so overworked, your questions and concerns may never be addressed. But don't give up working with your caseworker just because he or she may not have time to help. Take advantage of the free assistance and be grateful for whatever help you get. The important thing to remember is not to simply turn your case over to the agency, sit back, and do nothing while you assume that child support will ultimately be collected. If you do, you may never collect. Get personally involved and always assume that the agency caseworker will not be able to recover anything for you.

b. Agency history

Have you ever wondered why the government is involved in the child support collection process? If you have, a brief review of the history of child support collection agencies might answer your questions.

There was a time when collecting child support was given a low priority by the state and federal governments. The law recognized that a parent had an obligation to support his or her child, but it did little to assist with the process of child support collection. Indeed, there was little concern shown by the government over unpaid child support until after 1935, when the federal government created the Aid to Families with Dependent Children (AFDC) program as part of the Social Security Act. Gradually, the public began voicing objections about spending large amounts of tax money for this program while so many noncustodial parents failed to pay child support.

In the early 1970s, the federal government began debating the economic impact of tax money spent on public assistance for families that had been abandoned by a parent — typically the father. The result of this debate was the Child Support and Establishment of Paternity Act of 1974. That act created Title IV-D of the Social Security Act. You might be familiar with the term "IV-D agency" from dealing with your state child support collection agency.

The 1974 act imposed a mandate on states requiring their child support agencies to meet certain federal requirements. If they did not, they suffered a 5% reduction in federal support for their AFDC programs. This 5% penalty amounted to millions of dollars in lost federal support for most state child support agencies if they failed to follow the federal mandates. If a state's child support collection program was approved, it received federal funds for 75% of its cost.

Because of these incentives, state child support collection agencies got busy implementing programs to locate absent parents, establish paternity, and enforce child support orders.

Even parents who are not on AFDC could use the services of a state IV-D agency, but typically they would pay a fee to receive services. The logic behind extending child support collection services to all parents was that if a parent was not on AFDC, he or she could soon end up receiving AFDC if steps were not taken to collect past-due child support.

c. Agency overload

State child support collection agencies have been both a success and a failure. This may seem logically impossible, but consider this: the child support enforcement division of state IV-D agencies is one of the most utilized government agencies. If use and demand for service is the measuring stick for success, then state child support enforcement agencies are wildly successful. The Federal Office of Child Support Enforcement reported that its caseload for fiscal year 1994 was 18.6 million cases. On the other hand, these agencies were so overwhelmed with cases that they were either not able to serve, or failed to adequately serve, many of the people in need of their assistance.

For example, in Texas there are approximately 1,100 child support collection cases for every agency caseworker. There is no way that one caseworker can properly handle 1,100 child support collection cases in one year. If success is based on the ability to adequately serve all people who are in need of help, then state child support collection agencies have not been successful.

It is unrealistic to expect agency caseworkers to be able to collect child support from all delinquent parents. But most experts agree that state child support enforcement agencies could do a better job. Congress also recognized this need for improved agency performance and so increased the power of child support collection agencies with the 1996 Welfare Reform Act.

d. Increased agency power

One of the bottlenecks in the child support collection process has been the need for agency caseworkers to work with the judicial system when enforcing support orders. For example, if the agency sought to obtain a genetic test for proving paternity, it had to take action through the courts. The 1996 Welfare Reform Act has reduced the agency's reliance on the judicial system. The act directs states to create procedures that give state agencies the authority to take certain actions relating to establishing paternity, enforcing support orders, and modifying support orders without the need to obtain a judicial or administrative order. The actions that must be authorized for agency use include:

(a) Genetic testing to determine paternity

(b) Subpoenaing of financial information needed to establish, enforce, or modify a child support order

(c) Obtaining financial information about people employed, or receiving compensation from a state

(d) Accessing state records, including records related to marriage, birth, divorce, taxation, real estate, professional licenses, corporate ownership and control, partnerships, employment security, public assistance programs, motor vehicles, and corrections

(e) Accessing private records, including the computer records of cable television companies, public utilities, and financial institutions

(f) Ordering income withholding

(g) Securing assets, including interception of periodic or lump sums paid for unemployment compensation, workers' compensation, judgments, settlements, and lotteries

(h) Seizing assets held in financial institutions

(i) Seizing public and private retirement funds

(j) Imposing liens to force the sale of property and distribution of the proceeds

(k) Increasing monthly payments

It remains to be seen how child support agencies will implement their newly obtained powers. They will, however, be constrained by due process safeguards which must include notice to the payor regarding the action to be taken, an opportunity to be heard and contest the action, and the right to an appeal. Another important grant of power to child support agencies is a provision allowing them to transfer cases to other jurisdictions within the state without the need for additional court filings.

e. Tips on dealing with a state agency

Child support collection agencies are sometimes criticized for their failure to give adequate attention to their clients' cases. Given the large number of cases that state agencies must handle, it is clear that much of this criticism is unfair. Nevertheless, you may have heard some of the horror stories told by other parents who have turned their cases over to an agency caseworker only to see it die a slow death from neglect.

Typically, the complaint is that the case was turned over and initially worked on, but as the days and weeks passed with no money collected, the caseworker lost interest and eventually gave the case little attention. All but forgotten, it languished in the agency files for years with no money collected. Eventually, the frustrated parent gave up any hope of ever collecting the support owed to the children and stopped calling the agency to check on the case, another victim of the lost-in-the-agency syndrome.

There are things that you can do to avoid this situation. The list below is condensed from responses to a survey conducted specifically for this book in which all the state child support collection agencies were asked to describe the things that a parent could do to assist with the child support collection process. (A condensed checklist of the state agency survey responses can be found in Appendix 1 at the back of this book.) The following suggestions should increase your odds of benefiting from an agency caseworker.

1. Minimize agency homework

Remember how much you hated doing homework when you were a kid? Agency caseworkers have more homework than they can handle every day of the week. Do them, and yourself, a favor by limiting the amount of homework they have to do on your case. Inundate your caseworker with information. Give the caseworker everything you have on yourself, your child support order, the payor, and the history of your case.

The most important information to provide is a detailed description of the payor, including employment and assets. If the caseworker does not have to spend large amounts of time finding this information, it is much more likely that he or she will be able to use the tools at his or her disposal to enforce your support order.

Providing detailed information about the case was the most frequent suggestion given by agencies in the survey of effective ways to assist the caseworker. Remember the map that was suggested in chapter 1? It would be an extremely valuable tool in the hands of your caseworker. Make a copy of it, and all related paperwork, for your caseworker when your case is opened.

2. Act immediately

Don't procrastinate about contacting the agency for assistance. As soon as the payor is more than 30 days behind in making child support payments, contact the agency and request help. There are two problems that can occur if you wait too long. First, you allow a large past-due sum to accumulate, which becomes a psychological barrier to the payor. The payor may begin to think that you are not that concerned about collecting the past-due support and that his or her support obligation is unimportant. After all, wouldn't someone take action if the unpaid support is causing a problem? The payor may also become discouraged when the arrearage becomes large because it may seem as if the amount due could never be paid. In short, the payor's motivation to pay is lessened when you fail to take prompt action. Second, a delay in contacting the agency only serves to make the agency's job more difficult in many ways. The payor has time to move, change jobs, or fraudulently transfer assets.

3. Be the squeaky wheel

It's true that the squeaky wheel gets the grease. Keep that worn-out phrase in mind as you deal with your child support enforcement agency. Call your caseworker regularly and request updates on your case. If the caseworker knows that you will be calling, he or she will be much more likely to work on your case. The caseworker will want to be able to tell you that he or she has done more than just sit on your file since the last time you called. Try to maintain contact with a single caseworker. By doing so, your case will become more familiar to the caseworker and this may motivate him or her to regularly work on your case.

As you squeak, bear in mind that there is a fine line between an interested client and a pest. Be careful not to become a pest. If you do, you run the risk of hurting rather than helping your cause. The caseworker may get so tired of dealing with you that he or she either passes your file to another caseworker, which can only delay things, or avoids your calls and ignores your pleas for help.

Call on a regular basis, but remember that calling every day is unreasonable. As a general rule, a phone call every ten days to two weeks is about right. Throw in an occasional letter and you should be able to keep your case on the caseworker's mind without pestering.

4. Be patient, truthful, and polite

Patience is not the only virtue. There is also a lot to be said for truthfulness and politeness. You cannot expect your caseworker to aggressively work on your case if you are impatient, deceitful, and rude. Human nature dictates that a person is usually more willing to work for and help someone that he or she likes. Your caseworker will not like you, and will not be eager to help collect child support for you, if you call and complain about the job that he or she is doing and threaten to report him or her to the supervisor if things don't change.

No matter how angry you are about the lack of progress made on your case, do not take out your anger and frustration on the caseworker. Child support caseworkers have a very difficult job. They are overworked, underappreciated, and spend all day trying to collect money from people who often do everything they can to hide their whereabouts and assets.

If you become frustrated at the lack of progress on your case, remind yourself that your case is just one of thousands being pursued by the agency. If you want real progress to be made, you will probably have to do much of the work yourself and no amount of harassment of your case worker is ever going to help your case.

You can begin your dealings with the agency by writing an initiation letter, and then a follow-up letter.

(a) Sample case initiation letter

When you first make contact with your state child support enforcement agency, it is a good idea to send a case initiation letter along with any documents you would send to the agency. See Sample #3 for an example of this type of letter.

(b) Sample case follow-up letter

It is also a good idea to periodically follow up with your caseworker to inquire about the status of your case. By doing this, you keep your case on the caseworker's mind. You can also update the caseworker with new information and collection suggestions. See Sample #4 for an example of a follow-up letter.

If you feel your caseworker is truly neglecting your case or fails to take appropriate collection steps, contact a supervisor in the Child Support Enforcement office and request that your case be transferred to a new caseworker.

f. Private agencies

Using a state agency is not your only option when you need help collecting child support. A large number of private agencies now specialize in child support collection. Most of these firms operate on a contingent fee basis. That is, the fee the firm receives is taken out of the child support it recovers on your behalf and no fee is due unless it obtains a recovery for you. The fee is typically in the 20% to 30% range. Many private agencies require payment of an advance application or registration fee ranging from $50 to $150.

The advantage of using a private agency is that you are likely to get help from someone who is not overwhelmed by a large caseload. Another advantage is that your caseworker will have a financial incentive to work hard on your case.

November 12, 199-

Mary Parent
758 Bond Street
Anytown, MI 48900
(517) 769-0000

Bob Caseworker
State Child Support Enforcement Agency
19 Western Avenue
Anytown, MI 48900

Re: Mary Parent — New collection case

Dear Mr. Caseworker:

My name is Mary Parent. I am contacting your agency because my ex-husband, John Parent, has failed to pay child support owed to me under the terms of our divorce decree. The decree was entered on April 1, 199-. Initially, John made regular payments. However, he has missed several payments this year and has not paid for the past three months. The monthly payment is $400, and John is currently in arrears in the amount of $2,000.

I am enclosing copies of several documents that should be helpful in your efforts to locate John and collect support from him. From these documents, you can see that his Social Security number is 555-12-444. His driver's license number is G02-073316. His last known address is 123 Oak Street, Town City, Missouri 55678. I believe that he no longer lives at this address, but he may have left a forwarding address. He is self-employed as a drywall contractor and often has jobs in the Joplin, Missouri, area. At one time, he held a checking account at Last

1

National Bank in Joplin. He owns several vehicles, including a restored 1967 Mustang that is worth at least $7,500. I believe he may have also recently transferred money into his brother's name to avoid having it garnished.

I hope that this information is helpful. Please note that the enclosed documents contain much more information that could assist you with your collection efforts. I am willing to help in any way possible and will contact you in the near future to discuss my case. I look forward to working with you.

Sincerely,

Mary Parent

Mary Parent

enc.

2

December 9, 199-

Mary Parent
758 Bond Street
Anytown MI, 48900
(517) 769-0000

Bob Caseworker
State Child Support Enforcement Agency
19 Western Avenue
Anytown, MI 48900

Re: Mary Parent — Case Status

Dear Mr. Caseworker:

Thank you again for all the work you have put into my case. Even though we have not yet collected any money, I can see that you are doing everything that you can to help me, and I truly appreciate that.

Are there any new developments in my case? If so, you may contact me at your convenience to discuss them. I will be calling you in a few days, so maybe we can discuss your progress then.

By the way, an old friend told me that she saw John working at the new shopping center that is being built in east Joplin. Maybe we could find out who the primary contractor is for that job and intercept his payment? Let me know if you need any information from me in order to do that.

Again, thank you for your assistance, and I look forward to talking with you.

Sincerely,

Mary Parent

Mary Parent

After all, with most private agencies, if no recovery is obtained, the agency is not paid. If you hire a private agency, consider a small agency. With a small agency, you are more likely to end up with a caseworker who has an ownership interest in the company and, consequently, a vested interest in whether or not your child support is collected. Don't be shy about asking the person you deal with at a private agency about what type of financial incentive the caseworker assigned to your case will have. Ask this question before you hire the agency.

When dealing with a private agency, use the same tactics suggested above for dealing with a state agency. Provide large amounts of detailed information about your case. Follow-up with frequent and regular phone calls and letters. Again, be patient, truthful, and polite. When you hire a private agency, it is very important that you set a specific date after which you intend to withdraw your case from the agency and seek help elsewhere. That way, if the agency is not getting anywhere on your case, you can move on to another agency or work on the case yourself.

You should also clarify what fee the agency is to receive if collection results solely from your efforts, and not from anything the agency does. Most agencies have contracts that state that they receive a fee out of child support that is paid, no matter what the reason for the payment. If the agency is unwilling to modify this provision, you will probably just have to live with it.

Private agencies claim success rates of 60% to 70%. These rates probably reflect only the number of cases in which some payment is received, rather than the number of cases in which full payment is received. Nevertheless, a 60% to 70% chance of receiving some money is better than no chance of receiving anything, which is what will happen if you do nothing. For comparison, the recovery rate for state agencies, according to official statistics, is approximately 20%.

There are several ways to locate private agencies. You can look in the yellow pages of your local telephone book. You can also ask your state agency caseworker or lawyer for the names of respected private agencies. It may seem odd to ask a state agency caseworker for the name of a private agency, but remember that a state agency caseworker is likely overworked and would probably appreciate having your case turned over to a private party. In fact, many states are privatizing their child support collection process by entering into contracts with private agencies.

The best way to locate a private child support collection agency is to conduct an Internet computer search of World Wide Web pages. If you type the words "private child support agency" into any of the Web search engines, your results will include references for 20% to 30% of private child support agencies. You can learn a lot by browsing through these pages. After you have narrowed your choices to a small number, get their telephone numbers (typically they have toll-free numbers) and call the agencies to request references. If an agency does not give references, go on to another agency. If it does give references, call those references to find out about the agency.

The following private agencies may be of help:

Child Support Collection Center
728 Blanding Boulevard
Orange Park, FL 32065
Tel: (904) 282-2881

Child Support Enforcement
Toll-free: 1-800-801-KIDS

Child Support Network
1528 E. Missouri Avenue
Suite B-106
Phoenix, AZ 85014
Toll-free: 1-800-398-0700

Childsupportnet.com
1511 North Pines Road
Suite 394
Spokane, WA 99208
Toll-free: 1-888-693-7669

KIDS
3201 Cherry Ridge
Suite 300
San Antonio, TX 78230
Toll-free: 1-800-729-2445

Midamerica Child Support Collectors
Toll-free: 1-800-625-3729
(non-AFDC cases)
$95 registration fee
claims 70% success rate

National Child Support Network
Toll-free: 1-800-PAYKIDS
$49.95 application fee
claims 66.6% success rate

10

Modifying child support orders

Maps can become old and lose their value. If you tried to use a map from 1950 to travel across the country today, your trip would take much longer than necessary because you would not be aware of the interstate highway system, which was built after 1950. Therefore, you need to make certain that your map is up-to-date. Your child support order must also be up-to-date. To keep the information current, you may need to pursue an action to modify your child support order.

a. Stale orders

Remember when you could buy a candy bar for a quarter? Go to a movie for $2.50? Buy a new car for $5,000? Maybe you're even old enough to remember when children didn't care what brand of athletic shoes they wore, and a new pair

95

could be bought for $20. If you are the unlucky holder of a child support order entered when these prices were in effect, and your order has never been modified, you have probably been receiving substantially less than a fair amount of child support. Your child support order has gone stale, and you should immediately take steps to modify it so that it reflects the current cost of living.

It does not take long for a child support order to become stale. In fact, even if your order was entered within the last couple of years, it could still be stale. The reason for this is that many states have only recently enacted child support guidelines that are tied to the real cost of raising children. Before guidelines were enacted, judges could order whatever amount they felt was fair. Sometimes judges were ill-informed about the parties' financial standing or simply ordered an arbitrary figure that was inadequate to cover the cost of raising children. Now that the states are required to follow child support guidelines, there is a well-defined formula that judges must follow when entering a child support order. These guidelines are based on the parents' income. Of course, even orders based on child support guidelines can become stale if the payor's income increases substantially.

There are several things you can do to avoid being subject to a stale order. First, if your order was entered before the time that your state enacted child support guidelines, there is a good chance that you will automatically be entitled to modify the order so that it conforms to the guidelines. The fact that guidelines have been enacted is usually sufficient evidence to convince a judge that circumstances have changed since the original order was entered, and that it would be fair to modify your order to conform to the guidelines. Most state guidelines are structured so that they set a higher child support payment than the amount ordered before the enactment of the guidelines. In other words, your children could benefit greatly if you simply ask the court to modify your child support order to conform with current guidelines.

Another way to avoid having a stale order is to monitor the payor's income. Perhaps your child support order was entered while the payor was a college student and working only part time. Keep tabs on the payor's educational and job status. If he or she has earned a degree and gone to work full time at a good job, you should immediately take steps to modify your child support order so that it is based on the payor's new income. You can also monitor the payor's income by having your caseworker request income information from the payor's employer. A modification of the support order may be appropriate if the payor has had several raises in recent years.

The 1996 Welfare Reform Act contains a requirement that all states put procedures into effect for automatically reviewing child support orders every three years to make certain that they are based on current information. This automatic review, however, is limited to AFDC cases. If you do not receive AFDC, you may have to monitor your child support order yourself. Some states will probably enact automatic review provisions for all child support orders, including non-AFDC orders.

Any steps you take to bring your child support order in line with the current cost of living will probably be met with complaints from the payor. Be prepared to meet these complaints with information about how much more expensive it is to care for children since the original child support order was entered. For example, point out the increased cost of food, clothing, housing, school activities, insurance, entertainment, and the numerous other things you must directly provide for your children. If the payor still complains, ask if he or she would like to work at a job that held no prospect of ever paying more wages than when the payor started. This is, in essence, what happens if a child support order is never modified to reflect an increased cost of living.

b. Fraudulent orders

Stale child support orders are not the only orders that need to be modified. Some orders are inaccurate from the very day they are entered. For lack of a better word, let's call these orders fraudulent, even though there is usually nothing criminal about them. A fraudulent order typically comes into existence when the payor provides false or incomplete information at the time the initial child support order is calculated. The false or incomplete information can fall into two categories: stating a lower amount of income than is actually received, and, a total failure to disclose assets or income. For example, the payor might have submitted records to the court regarding his or her business accounts that failed to show the true amount of income he or she has received. Another trick is for payors who are employed by friends to ask their friends to create false income-related documents.

If you are reading this book while your divorce or paternity action is pending, you still have time to take steps to avoid being subject to a fraudulent order. There are discovery procedures available to your lawyer that should enable him or her to obtain the payor's income records. You should carefully review these records with your lawyer so that you can point out which portions appear to be inaccurate. Do not simply rely on the payor's statements about his or her level of income. Even though you may have lived with the payor and think you know all about his or her income, it is still a good idea to demand all income-related documents.

There may be some things that the payor may have held back or kept secret. Tax returns are very important documents to review. They should contain all income-related information. But even tax returns don't always tell the whole story. If the payor is self-employed, you should request bank account records, which may paint a more accurate income picture than tax returns do.

One advantage of formally requesting income information through the court is that a payor who lies about his or her income can be subject to perjury charges. Make sure the payor knows this. You can get this point across without being confrontational. The best way to do it is to simply provide the payor with every scrap of information about your own income and, when doing so, tell the payor that the reason you are making such a thorough disclosure is that you are very concerned about the penalties that could be imposed on you if you are found to have committed perjury by lying about your income. Tell the payor that your lawyer has made it very clear to you that if you lie about your income you could be charged with criminal perjury, fined, and even jailed. This should plant the seed in the payor's mind that withholding income information can lead only to trouble.

c. Reverse modification

The modification sword cuts both ways. That is, if the payor suffers a decrease in income or otherwise falls on hard times financially, he or she may be able to have the child support order reduced. This is entirely fair. Sometimes it is very obvious that the payor is in need of a reduction in the child support obligation. For example, the payor may have been involved in a serious accident that caused permanent disability. It would be fruitless, and indeed cruel, to oppose a modification under these circumstances. However, make certain that you are not the victim of a ruse intended to reduce the payor's support obligation. Use some of the same techniques described in the section on fraudulent orders to check the validity of the payor's claim of reduced income.

One important point to keep in mind if you are faced with an attempt to reduce child support payments is that the level of child support to be paid is not always based on the actual income the payor receives. As previously noted, most states recognize that the payor's *earning capacity* is equally important. In other words, if the payor is a physician who decides to quit his or her job and do volunteer work, it is likely that the judge won't allow this person to reduce his or her child support obligation. A parent will not be allowed to voluntarily reduce his or her income at the expense of the children.

Sometimes, a payor will attempt to reduce a child support obligation by threatening to seek custody of the children and then offering to dismiss the action if you agree to a lesser amount of child support. Do not fall for this trick. Child custody is not lightly changed. Unless you are doing a poor job of raising your children or an older child has requested to live with the other parent, it is highly unlikely that a court would change custody.

Consider requesting modification of a child support order if:

(a) The payor's income has increased

(b) It has been three or more years since your child support order was entered or last modified

(c) Your child-related expenses have substantially increased (e.g., a child has new and serious health problems)

(d) You learn that the payor understated his or her income when the support order was entered

(e) You learn that the payor failed to disclose a source of income when the support order was entered

11

Hiring a lawyer

a. A high-priced travel agent

A good travel agent can make the difference between an enjoyable trip and a trip you wish you had never taken. A travel agent can take care of the complicated details, such as purchasing proper airline or bus fare, reserving quality hotel rooms in the right cities on the right nights, and making certain that a good tour guide is available. A lawyer can serve as a sort of travel agent on your child support collection journey. A good lawyer should be able to give advice as to the best way to go about locating the payor and the most likely means of collecting support. Like a travel agent, your lawyer may also have connections with other people that can greatly increase your collection prospects. It is important to know how a lawyer can help collect child support, and how to hire and deal with your lawyer.

b. When to hire a lawyer

Have you ever heard the story about the young man, just out of law school, who moved to a small town to open up a law practice? He was the only lawyer in town. For several years he sat in his office with only a trickle of clients coming through the door. Business was so bad that his bank account was nearly empty. He was just about to give up the practice of law and go to trade school to learn how to become a plumber. He figured that would be the only way that he could earn a decent living. Then, another lawyer moved to town. Suddenly, clients were beating a path to his door to hire him to handle their legal work. His bank account swelled and he canceled his enrollment in trade school. The two lawyers lived happily ever after.

If you read between the lines of this story, you are left with the impression that lawyers stir up trouble and create business for one another. This is simply not true. Lawyers know that if they pursue a frivolous case, all they will be left with in the end are angry clients demanding to know why they did not warn them in the beginning that their cases had no merit. It doesn't take many angry clients to ruin a law practice.

Unfortunately, some people believe that if they hire a lawyer, the lawyer will do nothing but demand a hefty retainer fee and then pay little attention to the case. Thinking that they can save a few dollars by handling their own legal work (or ignoring it), they avoid seeing a lawyer and later learn that they could have benefited greatly from this help. Don't fall into this trap. There are certain child support collection problems that require the services of a lawyer. It is impossible to state exactly when you will need a lawyer to help with your collection efforts, but if you use a little common sense and keep the upcoming suggestions in mind, you should be able to make the right decision.

The nice thing about getting a lawyer involved in a child support collection case is that this type of case may not require any advance fees. Some lawyers will take child support collection cases on a contingent fee basis, just as private collection agencies do. That is, a lawyer will agree to take your case and be paid a percentage of what he or she recovers from the payor if, and only if, the lawyer actually obtains a recovery for you. In other words, you don't have to come up with money in advance, or worry later about coming up with money that you don't have. If a fee is to be paid, there will be a source from which to pay it.

Some lawyers may ask for an initial payment to cover court filing fees and other expenses, even when they take a case on a contingent fee basis. This is a fair arrangement, as long as the initial payment is not too high. This initial fee should be no more than $500 if your case is being pursued on a contingent fee basis.

A lawyer can be brought in at various stages in your child support hunt.

1. Pre-order lawyer

It is crucial that you have a lawyer before your initial child support order is entered. The reason that you need a lawyer at that time is that you need someone to go through the formal procedures necessary to get every piece of financial information from the payor. Your lawyer will be aware of ways that the court's power can be put to use to force the payor to disclose income information. You also need a lawyer to look at the entire financial picture of your case, interpret that picture, and present an argument to the judge as to the appropriate amount of child support that should be paid.

You may have been told that the enactment of child support guidelines has made determining child support a simple matter and that, therefore, a lawyer is no longer needed. Don't believe it. While plugging information into guidelines is certainly easy, the important part of obtaining a child support order is coming up with the proper numbers to plug into the guidelines. The old computer phrase "garbage in, garbage out" is a good way to describe what happens if you don't use the proper information when preparing a child support guidelines calculation. Garbage in, garbage out means that if the data you enter into a computer is garbage, the information it spits out will also be garbage. The same is true with child support calculations. You need a lawyer to make certain that the proper information is being used in your child support guideline calculation.

Help from a lawyer is also important before entering an initial child support order because of the long-term nature of the order. Depending on the ages of your children, you may have to live with your child support order for nearly two decades. A mistake at the beginning can be extremely costly. Suppose that you pursue your case alone and, because you fail to get all the payor's income information, your child support order ends up being set at $350 instead of $400. If your child is a toddler, and child support is paid for the next 15 years, you will receive about $9,000 less than what you should have received. If you make a $100 mistake instead of a $50 mistake, you will receive about $18,000 less than you should have. Clearly, then, spending a few hundred dollars to hire a lawyer to make certain that your child support order is correct is a wise investment. It becomes an even better investment if it so happens that the judge orders the payor to cover your lawyer's fees as part of the divorce or paternity proceeding.

2. Post-order lawyer

After your child support order is entered, it becomes less important for you to have a lawyer to handle child support-related matters. By that time, you could have a child support enforcement agency caseworker taking care of your case.

You might also have a private collection agency pursuing payment on your behalf. Indeed, you may be doing just fine with your own collection efforts.

If things aren't going well, you will have to consider hiring a lawyer to handle post-order problems. Generally, the problems fall into two categories: serious collection problems caused by an absent or unemployed payor, or, a need to modify the order to reflect the current standard of living or changes in yours or the payor's situation.

The first category involves the typical difficult collection case. Perhaps the payor is self-employed or simply refuses to find a job. If you and your caseworker have tried every collection trick known to mankind and have come to the conclusion that the payor will never pay the support that is owed, do not even bother hiring a lawyer. A lawyer cannot force the payor to go to work. (This may soon change. Under the 1996 Welfare Reform Act, states must create a procedure that would enable the state to request a court order that would require the payor to participate in certain work activities.)

The second category — modification of a support order — is more likely to require the services of a lawyer. Modifying a child support order usually requires filing court documents written in legal language. It also usually requires a court appearance and knowledge of how to respond to potential legal maneuvering of the payor. (Modification will also be affected by the 1996 Welfare Reform Act, which requires states to create a procedure to modify child support orders every three years.)

If you are having a hard time deciding whether to hire a lawyer to help you with your post-order child support problem, consider the following questions:

(a) Are you trying to collect a large past-due amount?

(b) Have you exhausted all the collection steps you can take on your own?

(c) Are you confident that your agency caseworker has provided all possible assistance?

(d) Is the payor represented by a lawyer?

(e) Can you afford the lawyer's fees?

(f) Do you need to modify your child support order?

If you answered yes to any of these questions, it would probably be a good idea to hire a lawyer. If you answered yes to more than one question, then you certainly need a lawyer. When you decide to hire a lawyer, remember that it is not a task to be taken lightly.

c. Finding a lawyer

Given the large number of lawyers practicing, you would think that finding one to work on your case would be easy. It is not — at least it's not if you want to find a good one who will give your case the attention it deserves and who charges a reasonable fee. If you're lucky, you have already gotten to know a good lawyer who has done satisfactory work for you at a reasonable price. If you haven't hired a lawyer before, be prepared to do some homework and legwork in order to find the right person.

There are do's and don'ts for hiring a lawyer:

(a) Don't hire a lawyer based on what you read in a yellow pages advertisement. These advertisements are unregulated and lawyers can put virtually anything they want in them.

(b) Don't ask your friend, who also happens to be a lawyer, to take your case. This is a sure way to ruin a friendship. You also run the risk that your friend has no experience with collecting child support, but takes your case only because you are friends.

(c) Don't hire a lawyer without meeting with him or her first to discuss your case. Any lawyer who presumes to know how your case should be handled, and what fee to charge, without thoroughly discussing your situation, should not be trusted.

(d) Don't meet with a lawyer without first asking whether he or she charges a fee for the initial conference. Some do, some don't.

(e) Do ask the lawyer whether he or she can provide you with the names of other clients for whom he or she has handled similar cases so that you may talk with them. However, don't be surprised if the lawyer tells you that this is confidential information that cannot be provided to you. Indeed, the lawyer *must* keep this information confidential unless the client has consented to being used as a reference.

(f) Do ask friends, relatives, and other people involved in child support collection matters whether they can provide you with the name of a good lawyer. Word of mouth is usually a much better indicator of the quality of a lawyer than are advertisements.

(g) Do call your local bar association and ask for the names of lawyers who handle child support or domestic relations matters. However, you must also ask whether the names of lawyers are provided on a random basis or whether the lawyers on the list actually have experience in those areas.

After you have done the work necessary to make an informed decision as to which lawyer to hire, you must turn your attention to how to work with your lawyer.

d. The squeaky wheel theory

Remember the squeaky wheel theory discussed in the section on dealing with agency caseworkers in chapter 9? The same theory is useful when dealing with a lawyer. Again, maintain regular contact with your lawyer by telephone and letter, but be careful not to become a pest. By maintaining regular contact, you will keep your file in the stack of priority files that the lawyer is working on rather than filing it away out of sight. One telephone call each week, combined with a letter or two a month, ought to be enough to let your lawyer know that you expect your case to be worked on.

Try to have some new information to give your lawyer every time you contact him or her. This will keep your lawyer from feeling as if you have no good reason to be calling. The sample letters in chapter 9 can easily be modified to be used as correspondence with your lawyer instead of with an agency caseworker.

Most of the other suggestions for efficiently working with your caseworker are also useful when working with your lawyer. In short, you need to keep your lawyer well informed about your case, provide him or her with all information at your disposal, and offer to help in any way possible. You must also have patience and be polite. Your lawyer will be much more inclined to work on your case, and take a personal interest in it, if he or she truly likes you as a person.

12

Good things to know

a. Last-minute packing

When you take a trip, it is always a good idea to take a few minutes before leaving to make sure that you're not forgetting anything. It's a good idea to do the same thing when you are trying to collect child support. Every now and then, run through some of the lesser-known issues and make sure that you're not forgetting something that could hold the key to collecting the child support money owed to you and your children. Some of these miscellaneous issues are covered below.

b. The importance of allowing visitation

This point has been made previously in this book, but it is so important that it is worth making again: if you allow the payor to have reasonable visitation with your child, you will greatly increase your chances of receiving child support. Any child support agency caseworker can tell you that a common reason given for failing to pay child support is that the custodial parent has been withholding visitation. From a legal standpoint, visitation and child support are not tied together. From a tactical, moral, and developmental standpoint, they are inseparable.

Think about it. If you were obligated to pay hundreds of dollars a month to support your children, but you were never allowed to see them, would you be motivated to make the payments? Therefore, as a tactical matter you must do everything in your power to see that the payor gets all the visitation to which he or she is legally entitled, and perhaps more.

It is hard to understand why some parents withhold visitation. In the absence of well-founded concerns about abuse or a detrimental living environment, there can be nothing better than interaction between a parent and child. Your child needs plenty of good, quality, one-on-one time with his or her noncustodial parent. If your child observes you and the payor interacting in a cooperative and reasonable manner, those observations will be a lesson that will carry over into the child's own life.

Not only does visitation improve your odds of collecting child support and benefit your children's development, it also is free babysitting. Raising children can be exhausting. You should welcome the opportunity to be away from your children for a few days at a time.

c. Bankruptcy

Child support typically cannot be discharged in a bankruptcy proceeding. This means that even if the payor files bankruptcy, he or she will still have to pay the child support obligation, both past and present. The situations in which child support can be discharged in bankruptcy are so rare that they will not be covered in this book.

Occasionally, a bankruptcy filing can actually favor a parent who is owed child support. A child support debt is a priority debt, which means that it must be paid before most other debts. Therefore, if the payor has property as part of a bankruptcy proceeding, there is a strong likelihood that the proceeds, or part of the proceeds, will be paid toward past-due child support.

Even though it is rare for a child support obligation to be discharged in bankruptcy, you should make certain that your child support order provides that bankruptcy will not end the support obligation.

d. Crossing state lines

At one time, a payor could frustrate child support collection efforts by moving out of the state in which the support order was entered. Jurisdictional problems and differing state laws made it difficult to enforce payment. Some payors would go to another state and pursue a one-sided court action that would result in a new child support order in a substantially reduced amount. This will be more difficult to do in the future because congress has mandated that all states enact the Uniform Interstate Family Support Act.

This act provides a much more effective framework for enforcing child support orders in other states. The 1996 Welfare Reform Act also contains some provisions that give guidance as to which of two support orders should be considered the effective order. This should eliminate some of the confusion that arises when there are competing child support orders.

Do not let your agency caseworker or lawyer convince you that child support cannot be collected simply because the payor has moved out of state. It is becoming easier to enforce child support orders against payors who have left the state where the child support order was originally entered.

If you are not receiving AFDC and you request location and enforcement services from your state child support enforcement agency, you may have to pay a bit more for these services if the payor lives in a different state.

e. Grandparent liability

The 1996 Welfare Reform Act contains a mandate that each state create a procedure whereby the child support obligations of minor parents may be enforced against either the paternal or maternal grandparents of the child. If the payor in your case is a minor, you might want to point this out to the payor's parents so that they realize they could be responsible for their child's support obligation.

f. Payors not in the country

Sometimes a payor who owes past-due child support leaves the United States to live or work in another country. Do not let this stop you from contacting your local child support enforcement agency for assistance. Many state agencies have agreements with other countries so that support orders are recognized as valid in those countries. If the payor works for an American company, you might be able to be paid through a wage withholding order even if the country the payor works in does not have an agreement that it will enforce an American child support order.

If you run into difficulty trying to collect child support from a payor who lives in another country, contact the Office of Citizens Consular Services, Department of State, Washington, DC 20520. This office should be able to give you information on how to enforce an American child support order in the country in which the payor lives. It may also be able to provide you with a list of lawyers in that country who are willing to work on collecting American child support. Finally, remember that the Secretary of State will be required to refuse issuing a passport, or revoke, restrict, or limit the passport of a payor who owes more than $5,000 in child support.

g. Don't let success fool you

A final tip as you begin (or continue) your child support collection efforts: don't rest on your laurels if you are fortunate enough to get paid for all past-due and current child support. Payors who become delinquent, and then catch up with their payments, often fall behind again later. Therefore, you should continue to keep abreast of the payor's location, employment, and assets.

You should also continue to subtly encourage good child support behavior by showing your appreciation to the payor for the payments, and by being reasonable with visitation rights. It is also a good idea to continue to keep a low economic profile so as not to make it appear as if the money is benefiting you, rather than the children. Keep your map up-to-date. Don't let your guard down. Collecting child support is a difficult task but it certainly is not impossible to collect what is owed to your children. If you prepare a good collection map, follow that map, and employ the techniques described in this book, you will greatly increase your chances of collecting all the support the payor owes.

Appendix 1

Child support collection
survey checklist

I prepared and mailed a survey to the child support collection agencies in all 50 states. The survey asked agencies to suggest the most important things that a parent could do when attempting to collect child support. The results of this survey, from the states that responded, are compiled in this checklist.

☐ Prepare and organize facts.

☐ Provide the child support enforcement agency with the most accurate and up-to-date information on the payor possible. This information includes:

- Social Security number
- Full name (first, middle, and last name, plus aliases)
- Date and place of birth
- Telephone number
- Last known place of employment
- Military service status
- Health or life insurance information
- Real estate information — address of any property owned
- Membership with organizations, unions, or clubs
- Driver's license and automobile license information
- Names of friends

- Names and address of the payor's mother and father
- Assets (e.g., bank accounts, retirement funds, investments)
- Identifying characteristics, such as height, weight, hair and eye color, birth marks and tattoos

☐ Establish legal paternity.

☐ Notify the agency of any changes in the circumstances of your case.

☐ Be persistent, truthful, and patient.

☐ Keep accurate records of payment.

☐ Take action to motivate the delinquent payor to pay, such as driver's license and business license revocation, civil contempt, or criminal prosecution.

☐ Try not to let a huge past-due amount accrue. Seek collection assistance immediately.

☐ Cooperate with the child support agency.

☐ Obtain accurate information on daycare and medical costs.

☐ Understand the law, procedures, and limitations.

☐ Include the payor in the children's lives.

Appendix 2

Child support collection map

Child support collection map
of

_____

Children

Child's name	Date of birth	Social Security number
_____	_____	_____
_____	_____	_____
_____	_____	_____
_____	_____	_____
_____	_____	_____

Support order

Date of child support order:_____

Name of court:_____

Court clerk's address:_____

Clerk's telephone number:_____

Judge's name:_____

Court case number:_____

Amount ordered paid:_____

Additional amounts for:

    Child care expenses:_____

    Health insurance:_____

    Dental insurance:_____

117

College expenses:_____

Other:_____

Has order been modified?_____

If so, date of modification:_____

Terms of modification:_____

Amount of past-due child support owed: $_____as of_____

Interest rate for past-due support:_____

Date of last payment:_____

Payor

Name:_____

Date of birth: _____

Street address:_____

City:_____State:_____Zip:_____

Home telephone number:_____

Social Security number:_____

Driver's license number:_____

Employer's name:_____

Employer's telephone number:_____

Employer's address:_____

Payor's monthly wage:_____

Other monthly income:_____

Payor's assets:

    1._____ Value: $_____

    2._____ Value: $_____

    3._____ Value: $_____

    4._____ Value: $_____

    5._____ Value: $_____

    6._____ Value: $_____

Payor's debts:

1._____ Amount: $_____
2._____ Amount: $_____
3._____ Amount: $_____
4._____ Amount: $_____
5._____ Amount: $_____
6._____ Amount: $_____

Professional license, if any: _____

License number:_____

Educational level and description of any education being pursued:

_____

_____

Is payor married?_____

Does payor have other children to support?_____

If yes, how many?_____

If payor cannot be located, the following steps have been taken to locate the payor:_____

_____

_____

If payor cannot be located, the following steps need to be taken to locate the payor:_____

_____

_____

Other information about the payor:_____

_____

_____

_____

_____

_____

Lawyer

Name:_____

Street address:_____

City:_____State:_____Zip:_____

Telephone number:_____

Date hired:_____

Reason hired:_____

Collection steps taken by lawyer:_____

_____

_____

_____

_____

Amount collected by lawyer: $_____

Collection method:_____

I can assist the lawyer by:_____

_____

_____

_____

Evaluation of lawyer's performance:_____

_____

_____

_____

Other recommended lawyers:_____

_____

_____

_____

Target dates for follow-up calls to lawyer:

1._____

2._____

3._____

Public enforcement agency

Agency name:_____

Street address:_____

City:_____State:_____Zip:_____

Telephone number:_____

Date contacted:_____

Contact person:_____

Collection steps taken by agency:_____

_____

_____

_____

Amount collected by agency: $_____

Collection method:_____

I can assist the agency by:_____

_____

_____

_____

_____

_____

_____

Evaluation of agency's performance:_____

_____

_____

_____

_____

_____

Target dates for follow-up calls to agency:

1._____

2._____

3._____

Private enforcement agency

Agency name:_____

Street address:_____

City:_____State:_____Zip:_____

Telephone number:_____

Date contacted:_____

Contact person:_____

Collection steps taken by agency:_____

_____

_____

_____

_____

_____

Amount collected by agency: $_____

Collection method:_____

I can assist the agency by:_____

_____

_____

_____

_____

Evaluation of agency's performance:_____

_____

_____

_____

_____

_____

Target dates for follow-up calls to agency:

1._____

2._____

3._____

Collection history

Chronological history of collection efforts:

_____

_____

_____

_____

_____

_____

_____

_____

Collection goals

By collecting past-due child support, I will be able to provide the following for my children:_ _____

_____

_____

_____

_____

After collecting past-due child support, the time that I formerly spent on collection efforts will be spent as follows:_____

_____

_____

_____

_____

Target date for collecting all past-due child support:_____

_____

Appendix 3

Child support collection survey

I prepared and mailed a child support survey to the child support collection agencies in all 50 states. The survey included the following two questions:

1. What is the most important thing a parent can do when attempting to collect past-due child support?

and

2. Do you have any other suggestions for a parent who is attempting to collect past-due child support?

The answers of the agencies that responded are listed below.

California

1. Obtain/provide Social Security number for noncustodial parent, and establish paternity early on.

2. Be persistent. Use all remedies available. In California, use the services of the district attorney. There is no cost and there are many techniques to collect child support that private lawyers do not have access to, e.g., driver's license and business license revocation.

Florida

We have used public education campaigns, high-profile enforcement initiatives, and procedural adjustments to make incremental improvements to the program. At the same time, we have been developing a "model" process designed to make a dramatic improvement in the way Florida collects and enforces child support.

We have worked to increase voluntary payments by working with private industry and other state agencies to implement programs that will increase voluntary payments without adding large numbers of new state workers for enforcement activities. These partnerships supplement, rather than supplant, the work of our employees.

Illinois

1. The custodial parent needs to provide the Child Support Enforcement agency with the most accurate and up-to-date information possible. The more information that the custodial parent provides about the noncustodial parent's whereabouts, the quicker and easier Child Support Enforcement can locate the noncustodial parent and begin the enforcement/collection process.

    Information most helpful in locating noncustodial parents: Social Security number, full name, date and place of birth, address and telephone number, and last known employment information for the noncustodial parent. Also military service information; health or life insurance information; real estate information and address of any property owned; information on membership in organizations, unions, or clubs; driver's license and automobile license information.

The custodial parent can initiate and persist with administrative or court proceedings to locate the noncustodial parent, establish paternity, and enforce child support orders. Initiation and enforcement of a child support order are contingent on the establishment of legal paternity. The custodial parent should notify the Child Support Enforcement agency of any changes in circumstances to his or her case.

2. Custodial parents should gather as many documents as possible about the noncustodial parent and have information organized and written when presenting this information to the Child Support Enforcement agency. So, knowledge of the noncustodial parent's information, preparation and organization of information, and persistence are key factors in increasing the odds of Child Support Enforcement collection success. (For example, one woman whose ex-boyfriend had left the country discovered that he had returned for a wedding, notified Child Support Enforcement, and the sheriff's police served him at the wedding reception!)

Custodial parents and families involved in domestic violence situations should determine whether their safety may be in jeopardy if they attempt to establish paternity and collect child support. Families on public assistance who are required to cooperate in the child support enforcement process should notify their caseworkers of any domestic violence situations.

Louisiana

1. The custodial parent should keep accurate records of payments. He or she may keep a copy of the payment article or a ledger of payment including the date and amount of each payment. This information will be needed if court action becomes necessary.

   The custodial parent should also keep as much current information as possible regarding the absent parent. This includes the absent parent's last known address, Social Security number, place and date of birth, place of employment, names of friends, and parents' names and address. This information will be helpful in locating the absent parent and bringing him or her to trial if needed.

2. The custodial parent should give the caseworker or lawyer as much assistance as possible to help in locating the absent parent and bringing him or her to trial. Usually the custodial parent knows before the caseworker that the absent parent has changed jobs.

Maine

1. Ideally, a payor shouldn't be allowed to accrue a large past-due sum in the first place. With the availability of immediate income withholding, payments should be kept up-to-date *if* the payor has a steady job and the immediate income withholding order can be served. In situations where this isn't possible, the thing to do is to identify the payor's assets and move against them as quickly and decisively as possible and to take other actions that are likely to motivate the delinquent payor to pay, such as license revocation, civil contempt, or criminal prosecution.

Minnesota

1. Keep good data. Cooperate with the child support agency.

Mississippi

1. Provide as much identifying information as possible on the noncustodial parent (Social Security number, date of birth, noncustodial parent's full name and address, last known address, and place of employment).

2. Do your homework. Find out as much information as possible regarding employment, assets, and property.

Nevada

1. Collect as much information as possible, such as full name and aliases, date of birth, Social Security number, residential address, place of employment, usual occupation, assets (property, bank accounts, retirement funds, etc.), and other identifying information such as height, weight, hair and eye color, and tattoos.

2. Apply with an IV-D Child Support Enforcement agency within the custodial parent's state for services such as location, establishment of paternity, establishment and enforcement of orders. The costs are usually minimal in comparison to hiring a private lawyer.

New Mexico

Get all information about the noncustodial parent. Be responsive to the agency. Be truthful and patient — collecting on child support orders don't happen overnight.

Rhode Island

1. Be able to provide the agency that will attempt collection with as much information on the absent parent as possible: correct spelling of names, Social Security number, date of birth, address, and place of employment.

2. Be able to document the unpaid amounts and periods of support due and unpaid, and be able to provide a copy of the most recent court order for support to the collection agency or Child Support Enforcement agency.

South Carolina

1. Provide any updated information on the noncustodial parent such as Social Security number, employers, and licenses.

2. Continued cooperation with the agency attempting collection for you. The custodial parent remains the most vital source of information in collection attempts.

Texas

1. All parents seeking past-due support should seek collection assistance immediately once a delinquency occurs. Too many parents wait years to seek assistance. This allows the arrears to accumulate to an

amount that may take even a gainfully employed noncustodial parent years to pay off, since it is unlikely that the noncustodial parent would be able to produce a large lump-sum payment. Also, with the passage of time, the noncustodial parent becomes more difficult to locate.

2. Be patient; the process can take longer than expected. This is especially true when the noncustodial parent is unemployed, has no assets, resides in another state, or simply can't be located.

Utah

1. Keep accurate records of all payments received directly. Obtain judgments on your own for daycare and medical costs.

2. If you have been on public assistance in the past, learn the rules regarding distribution of child support and be aware that the state might pay itself back first for arrears.

Vermont

1. Gather as much information as possible, understand the law and procedures (and the limitations), and have patience.

Washington

1. Stay in contact with the local child support officer and keep track of everything that happens on the case, and of every payment received. Try to obtain and maintain information about the paying parent and keep the support officer updated.

2. Do not try to keep the paying parent out of the children's lives — work to include the paying parent in the children's lives.

Wisconsin

1. Provide the child support agency in the jurisdiction enforcing the order with any available information about the payor's address or employment.

2. Consider whether local child support agencies have enough resources available to provide adequate services. If the agency has a caseload larger than it can handle effectively with the staff and technology available to it, the parent may wish to contact local elected officials to suggest that the jurisdiction devote greater resources to this important public service.

Appendix 4

Federal and state child support enforcement agencies

Federal Office of Child Support Enforcement
Office of Child Support Enforcement
Administration for Families and Children
370 L'Enfant Promenade, SW
Washington, DC 20447

Child Support Enforcement Division
Department of Human Resources
50 Ripley Street
Montgomery, **Alabama** 36130
Tel: (334) 242-9300
Toll-free: 1-800-284-4347
Fax: (334) 242-0606

Child Support Enforcement Division
Department of Revenue
550 W 7th Avenue
3rd Floor
Anchorage, **Alaska** 99501-6699
Tel: (907) 269-6900
Toll-free: 1-800-478-3300
Fax: (907) 269-6813/6914

Department of Economic Security
2222 W Encanto
PO Box 40458
Site Code 776A
Phoenix, **Arizona** 85067
Tel: (602) 252-4045
Toll-free: 1-800-882-4150
Fax: (602) 248-3126

Division of Child Support Enforcement
Arkansas Social Services
PO Box 3358
Little Rock, **Arkansas** 72203
Tel: (501) 682-8398
Toll-free: 1-800-247-4549
Fax: (501) 682-6002

Child Support Program Management Branch
Department of Social Services
744 P Street
Mail Stop 9-011
Sacramento, **California** 95814
Tel: (916) 654-1556
Fax: (916) 657-3791

Division of Child Support Enforcement
Department of Social Services
1575 Sherman Street
Denver, **Colorado** 80203-1714
Tel: (303) 866-5994
Fax: (303) 866-3574

Bureau of Child Support Enforcement
Department of Human Resources
1049 Asylum Avenue
Hartford, **Connecticut** 06105
Tel: (860) 569-6233
Fax: (860) 569-6557

Division of Child Support Enforcement
Department of Health and Social Services
PO Box 904
1901 N Dupont Highway
New Castle, **Delaware** 19720
Tel: (302) 577-4863
Fax: (302) 577-4873

Office of Paternity and Child Support
Department of Human Services
3rd Floor, Suite 3013
425 "I" Street NW
Washington, DC 20001
Tel: (202) 879-1416
Fax: (202) 434-9580

Office of Child Support Enforcement
Department of Health and Rehabilitative Services
1317 Winewood Boulevard, Building 3
Tallahassee, Florida 32399-0700
Tel: (904) 922-9590
Toll-free: 1-800-622-5371
Fax: (904) 488-4401

Office of Child Support Recovery
State Department of Human Resources
878 Peachtree Street NE
Room 529
Atlanta, Georgia 30309
Tel: (404) 657-3851
Fax: (404) 657-3326

Child Support Enforcement Administration
Department of Law
238 Archbishop F.C. Flores
7th Floor
Agana, Guam 96910
Tel: (671) 475-3360

Child Support Enforcement Agency
Department of the Attorney General
680 Iwilei Road, Suite 490
Honolulu, Hawaii 96817
Tel: (808) 587-3730
Fax: (808) 587-3775

Bureau of Child Support Enforcement
Department of Health and Welfare
450 W State Street,
Towers Building, 5th Floor
Boise, **Idaho** 83720
Tel: (208) 334-5710
Fax: (208) 334-0666

Division of Child Support Enforcement
Department of Public Aid
Prescott E. Bloom Building
201 S Grand Avenue E
PO Box 19405
Springfield, **Illinois** 62794-9405
Tel: (217) 524-4602
Toll-free: 1-800-447-4278

Child Support Enforcement Division
Department of Public Welfare
402 W Washington Street,
Room W360
Indianapolis, **Indiana** 46204
Tel: (515) 327-1800
Fax: (515) 327-1801

Bureau of Collections
Iowa Department of Human Services
Hoover Building, 5th Floor
Des Moines, **Iowa** 50319
Tel: (317) 281-5580
Fax: (317) 281-8854

Child Support Enforcement Program
Department of Social and Rehabilitative Services
Biddle Building
300 SW Oakley Street
PO Box 497
Topeka, **Kansas** 66603
Tel: (913) 296-3237
Fax: (913) 296-5206

Cabinet for Families and Children
Department of Social Insurance
Division of Child Support Enforcement
PO Box 2150 B5
Frankfort, **Kentucky** 40602-2150
Tel: (502) 564-2285
Fax: (502) 564-5988

Support Enforcement Services
Department of Social Services
PO Box 94065
Baton Rouge, **Louisiana** 70804
Tel: (504) 342-4780
Fax: (504) 342-7397

Support Enforcement and Recovery
Department of Human Services
State House, Station 11
Augusta, **Maine** 04333
Tel: (207) 287-2886
Fax: (207) 287-5096

Child Support Enforcement Administration
Department of Human Resources
311 W Saratoga Street
Baltimore, **Maryland** 21201
Tel: (410) 767-7881
Fax: (410) 333-8992

Child Support Enforcement Division
Department of Revenue
141 Portland Street
Cambridge, **Massachusetts** 02139
Tel: (617) 577-7200
Fax: (617) 621-4991

Office of Child Support
Family Independence Agency
7109 W Saginaw Highway
PO Box 30478
Lansing, **Michigan** 48909-7978
Tel: (517) 373-7570
Fax: (517) 373-4980

Child Support Enforcement Division
Department of Human Services
444 Lafayette Road
4th Floor
St Paul, **Minnesota** 55155
Tel: (612) 215-1714
Fax: (612) 297-4450

Child Support Division
Department of Human Services
515 E Amite Street
PO Box 352
Jackson, **Mississippi** 39205
Tel: (601) 359-4500
Fax: (601) 359-4415

Division of Child Support Enforcement
Department of Social Services
3418 Kaipp Drive
Suite South
PO Box 2320
Jefferson City, **Missouri** 65102
Tel: (573) 751-4301
Toll-free: 1-800-859-7999
Fax: (573) 751-8450

Child Support Enforcement Division
Department of Social and Rehabilitative Services
PO Box 202943
Helena, **Montana** 59620
Tel: (406) 442-7278
Fax: (406) 444-9626

Child Support Enforcement Office
Department of Social Services
PO Box 95044
301 Centennial Mall South
Lincoln, **Nebraska** 68509
Tel: (402) 471-9125
Fax: (402) 471-9455

Child Support Enforcement Program
Department of Human Resources
2527 N Carson Street
Capital Complex
Carson City, **Nevada** 89710
Tel: (702) 687-4744

Office of Child Support
Division of Human Services
Health and Human Service Building
6 Hazen Drive
Concord, **New Hampshire** 03301
Tel: (603) 271-4426
Toll-free: 1-800-852-3345 ext. 4427
Fax: (603) 271-4787

Office of Child Support
Division of Family Development
Department of Human Services
PO Box 716
Trenton, **New Jersey** 08625
Tel: (609) 588-2915
Toll-free: 1-800-621-5437
Fax: (609) 588-3369

Child Support Enforcement Division
Department of Human Services
PO Box 25109
Santa Fe, **New Mexico** 87504
Tel: (505) 827-7200
Fax: (505) 827-7285

Office of Child Support Enforcement
NY State Department of Social Services
PO Box 14
1 Commerce Plaza
Albany, **New York** 12260
Tel: (518) 474-9081
Toll-free: 1-800-846-0773
Fax: (518) 486-3127

Child Support Enforcement Section
Division of Social Services
Department of Human Resources
Anderson Plaza
100 E Six Forks Road
Raleigh, **North Carolina** 27609-7750
Tel: (919) 571-4114
Toll-free: 1-800-992-9457
Fax: (919) 571-4126

Child Support Enforcement Agency
Department of Human Services
PO Box 7190
Bismarck, **North Dakota** 58507
Tel: (701) 328-3582
Toll-free: 1-800-755-8530
Fax: (701) 328-5497

Bureau of Child Support
Department of Human Services
State Office Tower, 27th Floor
30 E Broad Street
Columbus, **Ohio** 43266-0423
Tel: (614) 752-6561
Toll-free: 1-800-686-1556
Fax: (614) 752-9760

Child Support Enforcement Division
Department of Human Services
PO Box 25352
Oklahoma City, **Oklahoma** 73125
Tel: (405) 522-5871
Fax: (405) 522-2753

Recovery Services Section
Adult and Family Services Division
Department of Human Resources
PO Box 14506
Salem, **Oregon** 97309
Tel: (503) 986-6090
Fax: (503) 986-6158

Bureau of Child Support Enforcement
Department of Public Welfare
PO Box 8018
Harrisburg, **Pennsylvania** 17105
Tel: (717) 787-3672
Fax: (717) 787-9706

Child Support Enforcement Program
Department of Social Services
CALL Box 3349
San Juan, **Puerto Rico** 00902-3349
Tel: (809) 722-4731
Fax: (809) 723-6187

Bureau of Family Support
Department of Human Services
77 Dorrance Street
Providence, **Rhode Island** 02903
Tel: (401) 277-2847
Toll-free: 1-800-638-5437
Fax: (401) 277-6674

Child Support Enforcement Division
Department of Social Services
PO Box 1520
Columbia, **South Carolina** 29202-9988
Tel: (803) 737-3134
Toll-free: 1-800-769-6779
Fax: (803) 737-6032

Office of Child Support Enforcement
Department of Social Services
700 Governors Drive
Pierre, **South Dakota** 57501-2291
Tel: (605) 773-3641
Fax: (605) 773-6834

Child Support Services
Department of Human Services
Citizens Plaza Building, 12th Floor
400 Deadrick Street
Nashville, **Tennessee** 37219
Tel: (615) 313-4880
Toll-free: 1-800-878-6911
Fax: (615) 532-2791

Child Support Enforcement Division
Office of the Attorney General
PO Box 12017
Austin, **Texas** 78711-2017
Tel: (512) 463-2181
Toll-free: 1-800-252-8014
Fax: (512) 834-9712

Office of Recovery Services
Department of Social Services
515 E 100 South
PO Box 45011
Salt Lake City, **Utah** 84145-0011
Tel: (801) 536-8500
Fax: (801) 536-8509

Child Support Division
Agency of Human Services
103 S Main Street
Waterbury, **Vermont** 05676
Tel: (802) 241-2319
Fax: (802) 244-1438

Paternity and Child Support Division
Department of Justice
48 B-50C Kronprindsens Gade
GERS Complex, 2nd Floor
St. Thomas, **Virgin Islands** 00802
Tel: (809) 775-3070
Fax: (809) 775-3808

Division of Support Enforcement Program
Department of Social Services
8007 Discovery Drive
Richmond, **Virginia** 23288
Tel: (804) 692-2458
Toll-free: 1-800-468-8894
Fax: (804) 692-1438

Revenue Division
Department of Social and Health Services
PO Box 9162, Mail Stop HJ-31
Olympia, **Washington** 98507
Tel: (206) 586-3162
Toll-free: 1-800-457-6202
Fax: (206) 586-3274

Child Advocate Office
Department of Human Services
State Capitol Complex
Building 6, Room 812
Charleston, **West Virginia** 25305
Tel: (304) 558-3780
Toll-free: 1-800-249-3778
Fax: (304) 558-4092

Division of Economic Support
Bureau of Child Support
1 W Wilson Street, Room 382
PO Box 7935
Madison, **Wisconsin** 53707-7935
Tel: (608) 266-9909
Fax: (608) 267-2824

Child Support Enforcement Section
Department of Health and Social Services
Hathaway Building
Cheyenne, **Wyoming** 82002
Tel: (307) 777-6948
Toll-free: 1-800-457-3659
Fax: (307) 777-7747

KIDS, THE LAW, AND YOU
Robert C. Waters, Attorney
$12.95

Here is what every parent, caretaker, teacher, and social worker needs to know (but is seldom told). Selected by the Parent Council, this is a complete guide to understanding and using the legal system to protect your children. It answers the tough questions about how the law affects children, and explains a parent's rights and responsibilities on everything from child custody to caring for children with serious medical problems.

Anyone who has come in conflict with a spouse, the school board, the medical community, the police, or the state over a child-related matter will appreciate the straightforward advice this book provides.

Questions answered include:

- What government benefits are available to help parents and children?

- What if I suspect my child or a child in my care is being abused?

- What if my child is missing or kidnapped?

- Can children "divorce" their parents?

- Can a biological parent take back an adopted child?

- What rights do surrogate parents have?

- If my child breaks the law, should I get a lawyer to help me?

FAMILY TIES THAT BIND
A self-help guide to change through
Family of Origin therapy
Dr. Ronald W. Richardson
$9.95

How to deal with family relationships is a problem that most people never solve. Our lives are complicated by family relationships. Birth order, our parents' relationship, and the "rules" we were brought up with can affect our self-esteem and relationships with spouses, children, and other family members.

This book uses Family of Origin theory and therapy techniques to help you improve those relationships and your own sense of self-esteem. Written in lay language, this easy-to-read, practical book explains how families function and how to find different and better ways of dealing with family relationships.

Step-by-step exercises show how to make contact with "lost" family members, how to interview relatives to get a clearer picture of how each member fits into the family tree, and how to apply the principles to your own situation and develop a more positive approach to all aspects of your life.

Professionals will find this book equally useful as a companion to their Family of Origin therapy sessions with clients.

PLEASE, LISTEN TO ME!
Your guide to understanding teenagers and suicide
Marion Crook, B.Sc.N.
$9.95

If you are a parent of a teenager, you should read this book. Suicide is one of the leading causes of teenage death, and is often completely unexpected. A teen who seems happy and healthy may in fact be desperately crying for help. This book speaks sensitively yet practically to this important issue. It covers learning to talk to your teen, using peer support, and finding professional help when you need it.

Questions answered include:

- How do I tell if my teenager is considering suicide?

- How do I talk to my teenager about suicide?

- What aspects of our family life may influence what my teenager thinks about suicide?

- My teenager seems normal — why should I worry?

ORDER FORM

All prices are subject to change without notice. Books are available in book, department, and stationery stores. If you cannot buy the book through a store, please use this order form. (Please print)

Name _____

Address _____

_____

Charge to: ❏ Visa   ❏ MasterCard

Account Number: _____

Validation Date_____Expiry Date_____

Signature_____

❏ Check here for a free catalog.

YES, please send me

_____ *Kids, the Law, and You*, $12.95

_____ *Family Ties That Bind*, $9.95

_____ *Please, Listen to Me!*, $9.95

Please add $3.00 for postage & handling.
WA residents, please add 7.8% sales tax

Please send your order to:
Self-Counsel Press Inc.
1704 N. State Street
Bellingham, WA 98225

Visit our Internet Web Site at: *www.self-counsel.com*